How to be ...
Positively Optimistic

Thank you for looking at this book. You're probably asking yourself ... WIIFM ... "What's in it for me?" Let me tell you.

You'll discover how to ...

☑ Stay positive more of the time

☑ Recover faster from setbacks

☑ Influence others to be more positive.

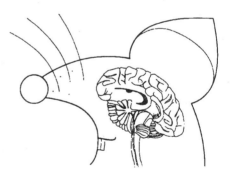

This is a self-help book for normal, healthy heads who want more growth and development.

You'll discover techniques to counsel yourself and make lasting change.

**Wherever the top is for you,
this book will help you get there.**

How to be …

Positively Optimistic

Ian McLean, PhD

HiPerform
Learning

First published in Australia, 1998

Reprinted 1998 Reprinted 1999

National Library of Australia
Cataloguing-in-Publication Data

   McLean, Ian B., 1998
   How to be Positively Optimistic

   Includes bibliographical references and index.
   ISBN 0 646 31012 7

   1. Optimism   2. Success   3. Life skills   I. Title

Cover design by Kristen Jean.
Art by James McLean, son of the author.
Printed by McPherson's Printing Group, Victoria.

Published by:

HiPerform Learning

6 Prince Edward Avenue, Mitcham VIC 3132, Australia
Phone (03) 9873 5517; fax (03) 9873 5377
International Phone 613 9873 5517; fax 613 9873 5377
E-mail   ellymclean@prospeak.com.au

For my wife Elly, whose optimism has borne fruit.

Contents

Introduction

How you'll get value from this book

This is a self-help book. It's for ordinary, healthy people who want to ...

* stay positive more of the time

* recover faster from setbacks

* influence others to be more positive.

You'll find clear, usable techniques for counselling yourself. You'll learn how to be more open to change and able to shift your thinking.

How does it work?

This book is ...

* easy to read

* meant to be used like a guide

* great to come back to when your going gets tough.

At the end of most chapters you'll find quotes which support the ideas in the chapter. Most chapters have a summary, drawn as a mind map. You can refer back to these maps to help you recall the main ideas. Each chapter also has a page to help you reflect and apply the self-counselling techniques. You'll benefit by thinking about your thinking, and how to make the ideas work for you.

You'll find out how to ...

❋ Talk to *yourself* when *your* going gets tough

❋ Talk to *others* when *their* going gets tough

with talk that's about ...

- optimistic views instead of pessimistic views

- solutions instead of problems

- action instead of procrastination.

Let's make sure we both mean the same things

Optimism: Disposition to hope for the best or to look on the bright side of things; general tendency to take a favourable view of circumstances or prospects.

Optimist: One who is inclined to practical optimism; one disposed, with or without sufficient reason, to hope for the best or think favourably of circumstances.

Pessimism: The tendency or disposition to look at the worst aspect of things; the habit of taking the gloomiest view of circumstances.

Pessimist: One who habitually takes the worst view of things.
Oxford English Dictionary, 2nd edition, 1989.

Affirmation: A statement repeated frequently to help change or maintain a current belief.

 # Look!

5 big ideas we'll talk about

1. We choose the way we think, most of the time.

2. Most of our feelings come from what we think.

3. Our feelings affect what we do.

4. Now, we can change the way we think.

5. So, we feel more optimistic and succeed more often at what we do.

Manufacturer's Warning!

There aren't many words in this book, so …
it's a short read.
But, there are lot's of challenging ideas, so …
it's a long think.

Acknowledgements

Some of the principles in this book were discovered by Dr Albert Ellis. He was a founder of rational emotive therapy during the 1960s. Dr Ellis used these principles as a psychotherapist and teacher. He saw them as an excellent foundation for a full and happy life.

You'll find his original ideas in *A New Guide to Rational Living,* 1975.*

Dr Martin Seligman studied optimism. His ideas added to the foundation laid by Dr Ellis, and have influenced this book.

You'll find Dr Seligman's ideas about optimism in *Learned Optimism,* 1990 and *What You Can Change and What You Can't,* 1994.

Many books are hard to read. Too many words and pages for most people. And no pictures! My son James helped make this book different with his witty images. Thanks, James.

*Reference details are on pages 153-154.

Chapter 1

Optimistic people have more fun

The greatest discovery of my generation is that human beings can alter their lives by altering their attitudes of mind.
William James (1842 - 1910)

It's a fact! Optimistic people are happier, healthier and more productive. They attract more of life's riches.

That's because they ...

* feel happier and more hopeful

* have better health habits, and catch fewer infectious diseases

* tend to live longer

* feel valuable and deserving of good things in their lives

* do better at school, university, work and sport.*

Optimistic people make good things happen for themselves and others. They keep on trying when their going gets tough.

They're more likely to make positive changes in their own behaviour, too. Which means they can grow and develop with new ideas.

That's a great way to live, don't you agree? And this is why it happens.

 **Optimism inspires hope and persistence.**

*Dr Martin Seligman, *Learned Optimism*, 1990

Mark Creasy is an inspiring example of hope and persistence. For 26 years he prospected for gold, much of the time in the wilderness 400 kilometers north of Kalgoorlie, Western Australia. Hot, lonely, dangerous work that few people would survive.

In 1978 he found his first 'fresh' gold in the region, but mining groups held temporary leases over the area. He waited over five years for their interests to lapse, then went to work.

Ten years later in December, 1993 a mining company paid him A$3 million and a bundle of shares for part of his prospecting interests. That alone was a prospector's dream result.

But he'd retained a 70 percent interest in some other areas, and kept working. Just six months later in May, 1994 he collected A$173 million tax free for these remaining interests. For Mark Creasy, life's riches now include financial wealth beyond the imagination of most people.

Twenty-six years of hope and persistence made him an 'overnight success'. He made good things happen where others had failed. Through heat, flies, isolation and danger he never gave up.

———— ✻ ————

We also attract life's riches when we hope and persist in pursuing our goals. Whether it's lasting relationships, education, travel, professional achievement, health, wealth ... hope and persistence help make it happen.

Pessimistic people have less fun

They often feel ...

> worthless
> > helpless
> > > hopeless.

So, they give up easier and get depressed more often.

 **Pessimism leads to doubt and procrastination.**

Of course, no-one is always optimistic and happy about every-thing. Unwanted things happen and we feel unhappy for a while. That's normal.

Optimistic people have highs and lows, yet they are in the high end more of the time.

By the way, you wouldn't want to be blindly optimistic because you'd ignore warning signs. That's dangerous when a steamroller is rumbling towards you.

Few people are always pessimistic about everything, either. That's just as well, because they'd often be depressed.

Pessimistic people have highs and lows too, yet they are in the low end more of the time. When their lows get deep, nobody wants to be around them. Their misery is catching.

Can we change 'the way we are' about optimism?

Most of us are somewhere on a line between extreme optimism or pessimism. The big question is – can we shift our thinking towards optimism and reap the benefits from a positive attitude more of the time?

Can we shift
this way?

➡ ➡ ➡ ➡ ➡

YES! Optimism is a skill we can learn

There's been extensive research with identical twins reared apart, and with adopted children and their natural and adoptive parents. It shows that less than half of our personality is inherited (except IQ which is possibly about 75% inherited). The rest comes from our environment and experience.*

Of course, we can't change our genetics. Those inborn tendencies are set for life. But much of our personality and world view were formed in the environment that shaped us. Family life, schools, national and ethnic culture, organisations we've worked with, people we live with now, our past and current experiences, and so on.

Optimism is a part of our personality which responds to training. We can learn the skills of optimistic thinking. We are not captive to our genetics and doomed to stay as we are.

So, our beliefs and attitudes arise in the interplay of our genetics and environment. We're not solid rock. With the right tools we can shift our beliefs, attitudes and habits of mind, and be more consistently optimistic. And as we've seen, we'll benefit greatly.

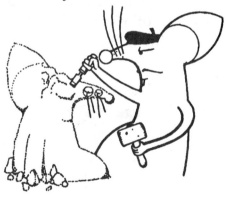

In later chapters you'll find some powerful tools to help you be optimistic and attract life's riches more of the time.

*Dr Martin Seligman, *What You Can Change and What You Can't*, 1994

> Progress is impossible without change; and those who cannot change their minds cannot change anything.
>
> *William James*

> Everything can be taken from a man but one thing: the last of the human freedoms - to choose one's attitude in any given set of circumstances, to choose one's own way.
>
> *Viktor E. Frankl*

> An optimist sees an opportunity in every calamity; a pessimist sees a calamity in every opportunity.
>
> *Winston Churchill*

> Nothing in the world can take the place of persistence. Talent will not; nothing is more common than unsuccessful men with talent. Genius will not; unrewarded genius is almost a proverb. Education will not; the world is full of educated derelicts. Persistence and determination alone are omnipotent.
>
> *Calvin Coolidge*

Summary so far ...*

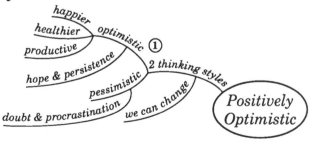

* This is the beginning of the mind map which you'll see develop through the book.

Pause, reflect and apply*

As you think about your personal and family life, how optimistic are you? If "0" is miserably pessimistic, and "10" is wildly optimistic, how would you rate yourself ... most of the time?

And how optimistic are you feeling in your public life... most of the time? What do others say about your optimism or pessimism?

What home, business, social situations would you like to handle more optimistically?

* Most people learn best when they apply what they see and hear to their own situation. You'll benefit if you pause, reflect and apply the ideas in this book to your life.

Chapter 2

Optimism is a catalyst

Resistance is thought transformed into feeling ... Change the thought that creates the resistance, and there is no more resistance.

Bob Conklin

Optimism is a catalyst that speeds everything else up. If we have a clear vision of what we want and the resources we need, then hope and persistence get us there faster.

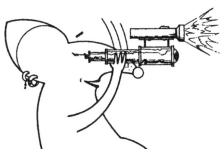

Vision
- a desired future
that motivates you

Resources
- talent, training, money, people, experience, etc

Optimism
- hope and persistence toward your vision

An optimistic view of our world helps us be happier and more productive, because …

what we **think** affects how we **feel** and then **act**.

So, optimistic thinking makes us …
* more hopeful
* more persistent
* more energised.

Pessimism is a saboteur
Pessimism fills us with doubt and procrastination. It can sabotage all the positive things that should help us achieve our vision.

For example, let's say progress is this way 👉 👉 👉

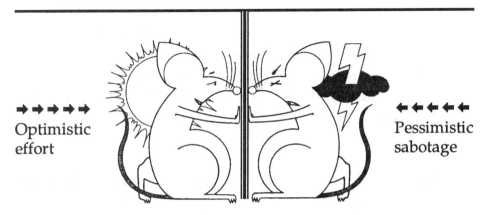

➡ ➡ ➡ ➡ ➡
Optimistic
effort

⬅ ⬅ ⬅ ⬅ ⬅
Pessimistic
sabotage

**Pushing harder and harder
doesn't help if ...**

**... sabotage and obstruction
just push back harder**

Some folks get on the left side and

push, push, push ... harder, harder, harder.

They have ...

* a stunning vision

* inspiring goals

* heaps of ability

* more and more hot training sessions and exciting meetings

* motivational arm waving

* affirmation cards and pictures

* people all around helping.

Yet nothing changes. They never achieve the potential everybody else can see. Because, they're pushing back on the right side with ...

● pessimistic views about themselves and their situation
● doubts and disbelief about their abilities
● rejecting success for themselves ... "I'm not worthy."

They reach a stalemate where pushing harder doesn't help. They have to remove the sabotage and obstruction in their heads. Then all the good stuff can work and move them ahead.

In March, 1994 Andre Agassi was number 32 in world tennis rankings. He was a flamboyant talent with an erratic history of entertaining performances but low achievement.

That month Agassi hired Brad Gilbert as his coach. Gilbert was a top ten player, in spite of his mediocre talent. His strength was in finding an opponent's soft spots and forcing them to play his game, rather than theirs. Gilbert saw through Agassi's cocky kid image and found hopelessly low confidence, focus and direction. He was sabotaging his talent with doubt and poor discipline.

Sports journalist Ross Wetzston wrote: "If Gilbert won matches with his head he had no right to win, he knew Agassi was losing matches with his head that he could have won."[*] When Gilbert's tactics were added to Agassi's talent, there was new hope and discipline. In the next year Agassi rose to number 1 and won the US and Australian Opens. He became the champion his talent deserved.

In Chapter 13 you'll find powerful tools to help you move obstructions that may be holding you back.

*Ross Wetzston, "Winning Ugly", *Inside Sports*, 1995

We have met the enemy ... and they is us.

Pogo, *Walt Kelly*

We are exactly where we have chosen to be.

Vernon Howard

The only limit to our realisation of tomorrow will be our doubts of today.

Franklin Delano Roosevelt

I've never seen a monument erected to a pessimist.

Paul Harvey

Summary so far ...

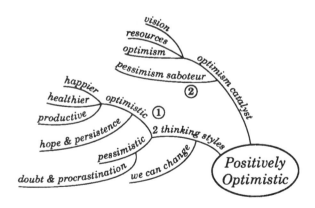

Pause, reflect and apply

What special strengths, beliefs and thinking habits are moving you ahead?

What sabotage and obstruction beliefs are pushing back? Such as: "I can't sell anything"; "Ugh, I could never speak at a conference like she does"; "I'm hopeless with people in powerful positions."

Chapter 3

Self-talk stories set our scene

Relentless, repetitive self-talk is what changes our self-image.

Denis E. Waitley

We've talked about why we're better off being optimistic. You might ask: "OK, that's great. But how do I become more optimistic, especially when things go wrong?"

That's what the rest of the book is about. You'll discover a track that's simple enough to remember and use when your going gets tough.

Now, here's a major idea.

1. **We choose the way we think most of the time.**

2   **Most feelings come from what we think.**

3. **So, we choose how we feel most of the time.**

That means our thoughts and emotions are linked. *We* are usually responsible for our feelings. It's not someone or something else doing it.

Sure, there are times when emotion seems overpowering, like when a loved one leaves or is badly hurt. But most of the time, in ordinary living, *we* create and keep our emotions bubbling or boiling. We do it as we talk to ourselves with **self-talk stories.**

Self-talk is the endless chattering inside our head while we're awake*.

It's running all the time. We're always questioning, explaining, judging, commiserating, blaming, congratulating, analysing, celebrating and so on.

We can listen to our self-talk and monitor our beliefs.

And we can change our self-talk to help change our beliefs.

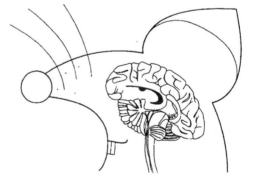

*The term "self-talk" was first used by Maxie C. Maultsby, *Help yourself to happiness through rational self-counseling*, 1975

16

We use self-talk stories to explain to ourselves what ...

✳ we think, feel and do

✳ others think, feel and do

✳ our environment does.

Some of our self-talk becomes automatic. It switches on 'without thinking'. Predictable self-talk stories run again and again.

We're always talking to ourselves inside our head. With our self-talk comes the **emotion** attached to our hopes and doubts.

If our automatic self-talk is pessimistic, then negative feelings quickly follow.

When we lock a self-talk story in our memory, we store it's emotion with it. Later, when we think about the story, we feel the same emotion all over again.

People who work or live alone spend big chunks of time listening to their self-talk. Like people running their own small business. And sales people, who may spend many hours alone between appointments. The quality of their self-talk can cripple or motivate them, depending on the stories they tell.

When I'm travelling to business appointments, I protect and nurture my optimism with uplifting audiotapes or cheerful music. No pessimistic radio news is allowed, because it can set off negative self-talk and feelings. I can't afford the effect that has on my performance.

Our self-talk stories can sound like ...

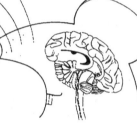

"Oh well, so what, I didn't need it anyway. There'll be other opportunities."

"You idiot! Why did you have to say that? Now you'll never get ..."

"Oh no! I messed it up again. I keep on doing that."

"Fantastic! I did it like I said I would."

"OK, so I lost face over that deal. But it's not the end of the world. I'll get it right next time."

"Wow! I'm getting good. That was a personal best."

"We pulled it out of the fire. If we'd done nothing, it would all be over by now."

What is an **optimist's self-talk story** like when their going gets tough? You'll find they:

1.   Stop destructive self-talk

2.   Create optimistic self-talk stories

3.   Feel more hopeful

4.   Act to affect the situation.

And, what is a **pessimist's self-talk story** like when their going get's tough? You'll find they:

1.   Use destructive self-talk.

2.   Create pessimistic self-talk stories

3.   Feel helpless and hopeless

4.   Do little or nothing to affect the situation.

That's a big difference between optimists and pessimists.

The choice is ours. We control what we think, most of the time. It's our choice whether we run optimistic or pessimistic self-talk stories, and there will be consequences from our choices.

My wife Elly and I worked on the coke ovens of the Great Lakes Steel Mill at Zug Island in the Detroit River, Michigan during a college summer break. Elly worked part of the summer in the fierce heat, fumes and dust on top of the battery of ovens.

Twenty tonnes of powdered coal was dropped through several 40 cm holes in the top of each massive oven. As it rapidly heated in the blazing cavity, gases ignited. Columns of fire 1.6 m high and 40 cm diameter roared out of the oven.

After every oven was charged she walked up to the columns of fire, each bigger than herself. Using a short steel rod she pushed a cast iron lid over each hole and sealed off the fire. All that protected her were light cotton clothes and gloves, respirator, and helmet with a clear plastic visor. Boots with wooden platforms underneath prevented her feet blistering.

This was a fearsome challenge for a person used to working in hairdressing salons and retail stores. It changed her beliefs about her courage and resilience.

Ever since, when Elly's times get tough, she switches on this self-talk: "Come on, McLean, you were a member of the United Steelworkers Union of America. And a member of the United Steelworkers doesn't give up! Get out there and do it."

This self-talk story has roused her hope and persistence many times. We all have success stories in our lives which we can draw upon. They can help us be more optimistic.

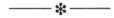

Your range of available choices - right now - is limitless.

Carl Frederick

We tend to get what we expect.

Norman Vincent Peale

When you expect things to happen - strangely enough - they do happen.

John J. B. Morgan and Ewing T. Webb

Summary so far ...

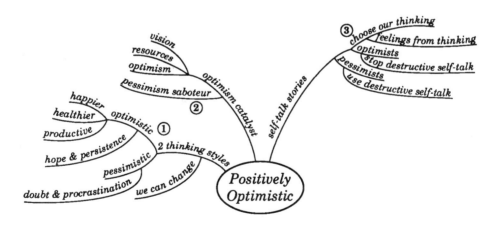

Pause, reflect and apply

Write down some of the self-talk stories you heard buzzing around your head today. Were they helping or hindering the happiness and progress in your life?

Chapter 4

Can we affect our emotions?

Feelings are what matter most to each one of us, moment by moment, and the feelings of people down the ages determine history, age by age.

Charles Birch

It's almost like we've got two minds*.

Our **emotional mind** tells us to take action. The word emotion comes from Latin that means "to move out, stir up, excite." So our emotions tell us to do something ... fight or flee, get closer, laugh or cry. These emotions *guide* our rational, logical mind. We don't make many decisions with our logic alone. There's almost always a feeling, intuition, a hunch involved.

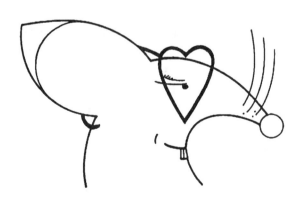

Our emotional mind
guides
our rational mind

*Daniel Goleman, *Emotional Intelligence*, 1996

23

Our **rational mind** *directs* our emotions. We think through a situation and our feelings, and decide how we'll act. That's a key feature of mature people. They've learnt to resist impulses to do things that would hurt their or other people's long-term interests.

Our rational mind
directs
our emotional mind.

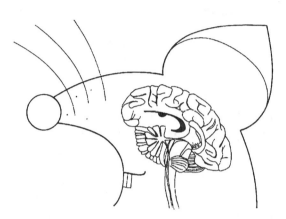

Much of life is a dance between these two "minds." Our emotions bring richness to life. Our rational thinking directs our feelings and actions.

Sometimes our emotions hijack us and we 'act without thinking'. It can happen in a crisis or threatening situation. Our brain snaps into action in a few thousandths of a second. We can't control when it happens or how we feel - at first. Moments later our rational mind catches up. Then we've got some say in *how long* we feel that way.

—— ✳ ——

Some years ago I experienced a huge emotional hijacking. My wife, Elly and I lived in Malawi, Africa with our four young children. The local political situation was difficult and we were uneasy.

At 2.30 am we awoke to a noise in the house. I rolled from under the mosquito net covering our bed and walked down the passage to check our children. Nobody stirred. On into the lounge room and a curtain was flapping. Impossible. All our windows were shut and barred against thieves. Under the window my bare feet crunched shattered glass. I whipped back the curtain.

Off in the distance I heard a screaming, roaring, bellowing rage. Then through the confusion I realised it was my voice and saw a man's face a metre away. He casually turned away, knowing I was locked in, and disappeared into the night with our bikes taken from an outside shed.

The rage was automatic and immediate. If I'd been armed he'd have died in the fractions of a second before my rational mind caught up.

Fortunately, emotional hijackings are unusual for most people. It's the passing parade of 'normal' life that we're dealing with most of the time. Then our rational mind more easily directs how we act in our relationships.

Realising what we're feeling when it's happening, and handling our feelings so they work better for us, is a major life skill we can learn.

That's a skill of optimists. They have the same problems and emotions as others. It's just that their automatic self-talk and rational mind direct their emotions so they feel more optimistic.

**We can't stop our feelings getting started,
but we can affect how long we feel that way.**

We can direct much of our emotion

Much of our daily emotion comes from what we think and believe about the world around us. We choose what we think about, and the emotions follow right along.

These aren't emotional hijackings. We direct these emotions by the ideas we let ourselves believe and think about.

✻ If we inflame ourselves about a team member, we feel resentful, angry and combative.

✻ If we celebrate achievement, we feel happy, fulfilled and hopeful.

✻ If we calmly solve a tangled problem, we feel satisfied, pleased and confident.

That's because much of our emotions come from what we choose to think and believe.

Realising what we're feeling when it's happening and directing it, is a major life skill.

We don't get upset; we upset ourselves

When we hear ourselves saying …

"※✱※✱ … You make me so mad."

"He's an idiot! ✱✱※ … He makes me sick!"

"This stupid ※✱✱ company really gets up my nose"

… then we're putting responsibility for our feelings onto someone else. The fact is, we're choosing to think explosive ideas that are guaranteed to send our emotions through the roof.

It's what's going on in *our head* that affects *our emotions*.

While judging and blaming people might give us short-term entertainment, it won't help us solve problems and get on with happy living.

We keep emotions going by what we think

Experienced parents know how to settle down a tearful child. Just distract them with a new interest.

Nothing much changes as we grow up. If we keep judging and blaming, adding fuel with violent language, telling our hot self-talk story to anyone who'll listen, guess what? The hot emotion keeps steaming and boiling. We stay mad and get to enjoy it. Meanwhile, life passes us by and opportunities are lost.

We get mad and stay mad,

or get happy and stay happy,

mostly by what we think.

What's wrong with emotions anyway?

Nothing, when they're not wrecking our quality of life.

People with flat emotions live pretty flat lives. Their lives are like chalk - dry, plain, uninspiring, colourless ... only good for smudging other people's lives.

Volatile, explosive emotion can be self-destructive too. It's hard work for us and everyone around us. Always getting in and out of boiling mud pools, splashing, scorching, sticking ... burning our relationships.

There's a lot of room between these extremes to live healthy, happy and productive lives. We can live rich and vibrant emotional lives without self-destructing and causing needless pain to ourselves and others.

Optimistic people choose to spend most of their lives on the energetic, hopeful, active side of their emotions.

What has optimism got to do with our emotions?

The way we think affects the way we feel. Optimistic beliefs and thinking help us feel hopeful and happy.

Optimistic thinking helps us feel hopeful, so we're more likely to act and ...

make things happen.

Pessimistic thinking makes us feel hopeless, so we're less likely to act, and ...

nothing much happens.

Optimistic thinking is more likely to get you what you want. Because, you feel like acting ... to make it happen!

31

> There is nothing either good or bad, but thinking makes it so.
>
> *William Shakespeare*
>
> Men are disturbed, not by the things that happen, but by their opinion of the things that happen.
>
> *Epictetus*
>
> (Hope is) believing you have both the will and the way to accomplish your goals, whatever they may be.
>
> *C. R. Snyder*

Summary so far ...

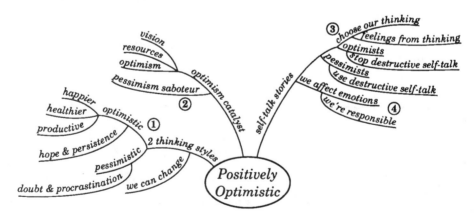

Pause, reflect and apply

Do you recall events that have been emotional hijackings in your life?

What self-talk patterns do you use to upset yourself?

Chapter 5

Helplessness and pessimism

> Any fact facing us is not as important as our attitude toward it, for that determines our success or failure.
>
> *Norman Vincent Peale*

During the 1960s, researchers discovered that some dogs would learn that they were helpless in certain experiments. When there was nothing the dogs could do to remove their discomfort, they gave up and suffered it. They had learned helplessness.*

Later it was found that some people learn helplessness too. When they believe they are helpless, some people get pessimistic about the future. Next thing, they slip into procrastination and inactivity.

If we believe that ...

● nothing I do helps now; and
● nothing I do will help in the future

... then we're likely to give up now and

take no action

---

*Dr Martin Seligman, *Learned Optimism*, 1990

People can learn helplessness in two ways.

No control

If we believe we've got no control over our situation, we can slip into helplessness and pessimism.

This happens in some organisations that run a command and control culture. Some people at the top prevent front line people from making decisions and expect them to work like robots. Of course, robots are helpless. Soon the front line people feel helpless, give up hope, and work by the hour or quit.

No wins

When we see ourselves losing in spite of our best efforts, we can slide into helplessness, too. "Nothing I do is good enough. I can't make a difference."

Competitive sport is fertile ground for this problem. There must be winners and losers. And the outcome may be seen and discussed by millions, including savage media critics.

Elite tennis players sometimes look crushed when they believe they are helpless in a match - head down, distraught faces, 'racquet abuse', language.

Elephant trainers use 'no control, no wins' and helplessness to train these powerful animals. Evidently they tie youngsters to a stake with a heavy metal chain. Try as they might, the young elephant cannot budge the stake or snap the chain. They are totally helpless.

This belief in their helplessness becomes so complete that an adult can be restrained with a light rope. As soon as it feels the restraining pressure, it stops pulling. We know it could break the rope. It believes not, gives up and takes no action.

Some people don't quit

The result of competition between people of similar talent and fitness can all hinge on what's going on in their heads. Helplessness can lead to hopelessness - and that's the end of the match.

We all know some people who *don't* give up, even when they're in 'no control' or 'no wins' situations. They persist against the evidence and the odds. No quitting. Kieren Perkins' Gold Medal win in the '96 Olympic 1500 m freestyle swim shows he's this kind of person.

What makes them different? It's a lot to do with their self-talk stories. And champion self-talk can be learnt.

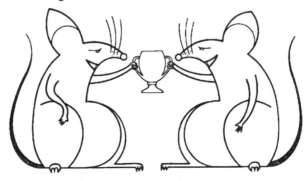

Learn how to think more optimistically

You'll recall this is a self-help book for ordinary, healthy people who want to ...

* stay positive more of the time

* recover faster from setbacks

* influence others to be more positive.

Which means they'll attract more of life's riches.

In the following chapters you'll find practical ideas to help you do that. You'll learn a memory aid that looks like this:*

A	=	**Action**
B	=	**Belief**
C	=	**Consequence**
D	=	**Dispute**
E	=	**Energise**

It's a way to shift our thinking to be more real and optimistic. And, it's simple enough that you can think of it when your going gets tough.

* This model was started by Dr Albert Ellis, (see *A New Guide to Rational Living*, 1975): Dr Martin Seligman developed the model further in *Learned Optimism*, 1990.

Things turn out best for the people who make the best of the way things turn out.

John Wooden

Whether you think you can or you can't - you are right.

Henry Ford

Any fact facing us is not as important as our attitude toward it, for that determines our success or failure.

Norman Vincent Peale

I never see failure as failure, but only as the game I must play to win.

Tom Hopkins

Summary so far ...

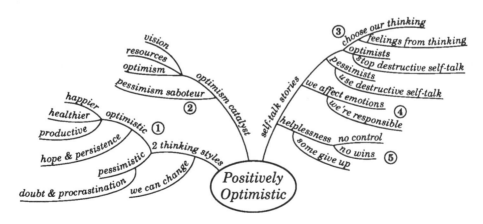

Pause, reflect and apply

Have you seen or experienced the belief of helplessness in your life, or in people around you? What was the outcome?

Chapter 6

A = Action

☞ **A = Action**

 B = Belief

 C = Consequence

 D = Dispute

 E = Energise

> ... the facts are always friendly. Every bit of evidence one can acquire, in any area, leads one that much closer to what is true.
>
> *Carl Rogers*

When some action or event happens in our world, we create our unique self-talk story about it.

Each of us perceives the world through our own 'glasses' or 'filters'. They develop over the years from our thinking style, education, culture, profession, life philosophy, experiences, and so on. Our filters help determine our view of the world.

That means people can perceive the same action in different ways. They create their unique self-talk story.

Our personal filters can affect how optimistic or pessimistic we feel, because they feed ideas into our beliefs.

We're more likely to enjoy happy, healthy and productive lives when we perceive the world as it really is. We've got more chance of dealing with it successfully.

Analysing and reasoning

Some folks prefer to analyse and reason to understand events. They break the action into facts and pieces, pull it apart, put it back together again – and form a view.

Feeling and intuition

Some folks prefer to feel it out with their intuition and senses. They rely a lot on how they feel about the action – and form a view.

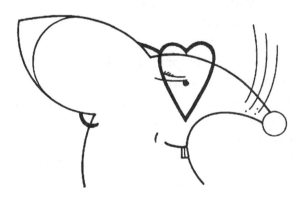

Bit of each

Some folks do a bit of each. They feel it out, then analyse and think about it – and form a view.

Each group sees the situation from different viewpoints. It's no wonder they can form different views about the same situation.

Reality check

We'd better do a reality check before we get hung up on our view.

We never know the whole story

Even the people involved may not realise what's going on in their own heads.

We're better off if we check our thinking and feeling with reality. Maybe ask other people about their thinking and feeling, get more information, and seek other views than ours.

Otherwise, our view can be fantasy, even though it seems OK to us.

The facts are always friendly*

We're always better off knowing the facts about an action or event. Then we can think and feel from a better starting point. If we get a false start to our thinking and feeling about an action, we're more likely to finish up with a false view.

*Dr Carl Rogers, *On Becoming a Person*, 1967

The more facts and fewer assumptions we start with, the better our view. It's like the saying in the computer industry ...

GIGO – garbage in, garbage out

Being real

Dr Abraham Maslow* was a famous American psychologist. Lots of people know him for his heirarchy of needs.

Dr Maslow wanted to know what made extremely creative and mature people so remarkable. Most of the people he studied were in their 50s to 70s. He called these people self-actualisers.

Think of an exceptional person you know who has worked hard for many years to climb towards their true potential.

Dr Maslow called this life-long journey 'self-actualising'. It means to make actual or real what was before only potential within us.

*Dr Abraham Maslow, *Motivation and Personality*, 1970

The journey is life-long because our potential is so great. Self-actualising people never stop learning and growing, as long as their minds keep working well.

Dr Maslow found that self-actualising people have a better perception of reality. They are able to see events as they are, rather than as they or their cultural group want them to be.

Being transparently real

'What you see is what you get.' No masks. No mind games. Values and behaviours are one.

I find transparently real people a joy to be with. It doesn't matter whether or not we agree. That's not the point. It's the communication that's a pleasure.

People who won't disclose their real thoughts, intentions or feelings leave me wondering. I don't have enough facts, so then I have to guess. After half a century of guessing intentions my success rate is still poor. Misunderstanding is almost inevitable.

It's much easier to be optimistic about people when they are transparently real.

> ... the facts are always friendly. Every bit of evidence one can acquire, in any area, leads one that much closer to what is true.
>
> *Carl Rogers*

Summary so far ...

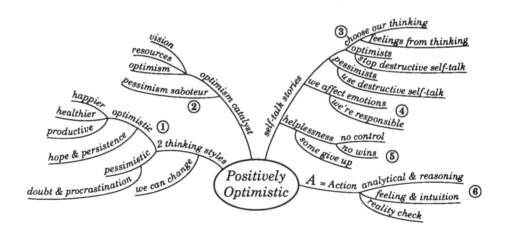

Pause, reflect and apply

How do you look at events that happen around you? Do you mostly feel it out, analyse it, or a bit of each?

Would you benefit from more reality checks along the way?

Positively Optimistic

Chapter 7

B = Belief

A = Action
☞ B = Belief
C = Consequence
D= Dispute
E = Energise

You and I do not see things as they are. We see things as we are.

Herb Cohen

During a conference speaking trip to South Africa I stayed in a Johannesburg hotel for several days. It was quiet in the evenings and I watched some of the 24 hour news available in the hotel – BBC, CNN and SKY.

Sombre announcers reported the world's misery. Often it was murderous conflict between groups with opposing views of the same situation. People who had formed their views and would destroy each other rather than challenge or change their beliefs.

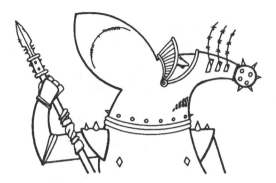

Many people get locked into their beliefs and will not change. Perhaps they fear ...

* loss of face with important people in their lives

* being seen as inconsistent, weak or unstable

* loss of feeling right, chosen, saved, unique, accepted, certain, safe.

Of course, we can't be changing our beliefs all the time. We need to be fairly stable to get along in life. And we have deeply held values and hopes that sustain us.

But we suffer when we hang onto beliefs that are harmful to others, self-destructive, or simply past their use-by date. Opportunities for growth and happiness can slip through our fingers.

The further we stray and stay away from reality, the less we are able to deal with the real world.

It's a bit like the blind mice and the elephant. Each mouse thought it knew what it was dealing with. But each came to a completely different view about the same creature.

We can be happier, healthier and more productive if we accept that ...

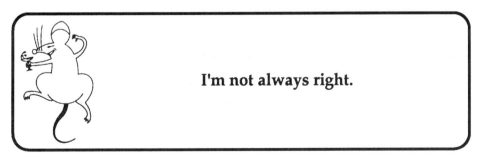

I'm not always right.

Sure, that's easy to accept when the situation is not important to us. But when there's a threat to our interests or value judgements, it's not so easy to admit that ...

Maybe my view is not *the* view.

People who can say these words in their self-talk and mean them, can allow themselves and others to grow. Often they open a window to greater happiness.

These words don't make us any less of a person. After all, our view may not be *the* view because ...

* we don't know everything about a situation
* we misread other people's intentions
* other people have different values and beliefs, and form different views.

Our life can be an exciting journey of discovery when we can deeply accept that ...

My view is one view.
There could be a better view.
It's OK to change my view.

In some technical situations the facts are so well known, the evidence so strong, that it's unlikely there's a better view. But in people situations, we usually have something to learn.

During the 1970s I attended universities in the United States. Through eight years and three degrees, the university system taught me to be right. All the time. If I was wrong, my grades would drop and put my scholarship at risk. That got my attention, because it was paying my tuition fees. I was supporting our family and going to school full time, so every dollar counted.

I faced countless science exam questions that were written so there was one right answer. So, I focused on always getting the instructor's right answer. Our family finances depended on it.

Eight years of being right in a highly competitive university system had two unfortunate side effects. I felt like I'd lost my creativity. But worse, I came to believe that my judgement was virtually always right, in everything. Dangerous stuff, because in life there are few 'right' answers.

It took years to unlearn this delusion. And more years to accept that my view is one view, there could be a better view, and it's OK to change my view. Now I am free ... and creative.

Age, power, exceptional talent, top performance in some field can lead us to believe that our view is *the* view. Then we're likely to feel frustrated and pessimistic when things don't go the way we 'know' they should. Next thing, we're not much fun to be around.

A readiness to change our view is at the heart of growth. Without change we're locked in a cell of beliefs. The world ignores our self-imposed prison and leaves us behind.

Appearances are deceptive.

Aesop

We are all captives of the pictures in our head - our belief that the world we have experienced is the world that really exists.

Walter Lippman

Summary so far ...

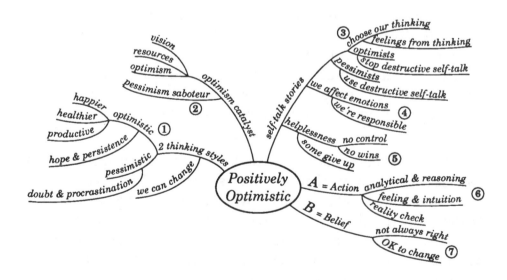

Pause, reflect and apply

Some folks resist changing their view, fearing a loss of face. As more people know their view, and the longer they've held it, the harder it is to change. How do you feel about the statement: "My view is one view. There could be a better view. It's OK to change my view."

Look!

Chapters 8, 9 and 10 describe common pessimistic thinking. The reason they are included in a book on positive optimism is to make us more aware of pessimistic ideas. When we hear this stuff in our self-talk or in others' conversations, we're more able to recognise it for what it is.

Chapter 8   **Belief ... Irrational beliefs we love and cherish**
These are big assumptions about life in general.

Chapter 9   **Belief ... Sad and sorry self-talk stories**
These are pessimistic ways of viewing specific events.

Chapter 10   **Belief ... Super self-talk stories**
These are three dimensions in which we explain our experiences to ourselves - time, place and cause. You'll see both pessimistic and optimistic explanations in this chapter.

As you read these chapters, you may recognise habits of your own. Be kind to yourself. It's a learning experience.

Chapter 8

Belief ...
Irrational beliefs
we love and cherish

The fact that an opinion has been widely held is no evidence
whatever that it is not utterly absurd ...

Bertrand Russell

In Chapter 4 we heard about our emotional and rational minds.
Ideally, our emotional mind *guides* the rational mind. And our
rational mind *directs* the emotional mind.

Sometimes we hold beliefs about life in general which are not
rational. They cannot be defended with reason. Perhaps they are
based on cultural traditions, false assumptions, little evidence, etc.
But they appeal to our emotions and sound reasonable ... to us.

So we love, cherish and defend them for years, decades, even
our lifetime. All the time they cause self-defeating emotions and
behaviours. And there are consequences for us and people in our
lives.

The Top 7 Hit Parade of Irrational Beliefs

Several people have made hit parades of popular irrational
beliefs. Dr Mel Witmer made a list of seven favourites from the
writings of other people and his experience as a psychologist*.
They're about life in general. Let's look at them.

*Dr Melvin Witmer, *Pathways to Personal Growth*, 1985

1. Life must be fair ... especially for me.

This means our health, people, politics, the weather, should all conform with our beliefs, needs and wants.

"Whoever said life is fair?" we might ask. The defence of 'basic human rights' is very recent in human history. The 'right' of political empires to invade, kill, plunder and dictate was widely accepted until the last few decades.

It's tough when it gets personal. If we're retrenched after years of service and sacrifice, exemplary friends are randomly struck by painful disease, innocent family members get hurt in senseless accidents ... "It's not fair!" jumps into our minds.

Of course fairness gets the best result for most people in the long term. Trouble is, everybody defines fairness through their self-interest, values and preferences. If we always insist on fairness as we perceive it, we'll often be disappointed. What we *can* do is face reality, get on with life and work to make things better.

2. If I don't get love, approval and admiration from people, then I'm worthless.

Believe this and we're on a roller coaster of pride and despair. Other people decide our worth as a person. So, we must be all things to all people. In the end, we become a nonentity whose values and beliefs are dictated by the moment.

Former US President Jimmy Carter became known for holding the view of the last person he'd spoken to. True or not, this reputation helped lose him re-election.

Sure, we all need the love and acceptance of a few significant people. Beyond that we can relate with people as they are, and ask no more than that.

3. When I make a mistake it's awful, terrible and catastrophic.

Some competent people believe that everything they do must be perfect. Their self-worth depends on it.

People who are paid to give advice can get hung up on this. Like lawyers, market analysts, dentists. Next thing, professional pride leaps into action to noisily defend their position.

Public speaking strikes terror into many people. Fear of making a mistake in front of a crowd is a big part of it.

Since we're unlikely to do new things perfectly, then it's safest to do nothing new. This is a recipe for underachieving and stalled growth. But there's no risk of mistakes.

High achievers make more mistakes because they do more new things. They discover pathways to success by eliminating mistakes. They have the courage to get it wrong, in order to get it right.

4. I can't do that.

This irrational belief keeps us from trying things that are well within our potential, given our talents and opportunities.

"I can't" may come from past failures. Or perhaps in a past environment no-one expected us to achieve much, so we came to believe we couldn't. Either way, we allow the past to dictate our present feelings and behaviour.

In Queensland I looked at the steep, fast waterslide and said: "I can't do that!" So, I tried the gentle, slower one. Got some confidence. Then I slid 80 km per hour down the steep, fast one.

When we move from "I can't" to "I can try", we can have small victories. Next thing, "I can".

5. **Problems go away when I ignore them.**

That's true sometimes. Like the old adage: 'Sleep on it; things won't seem so bad in the morning'. Our emotions seem to settle and we see things more clearly.

However, it's irrational to ignore the reality of entrenched problems. Nothing changes and our refusal to confront them delays our growth and achievement.

A close friend in her 80's had been bleeding on and off for nearly two years. Too shy, too private to get it checked. The problem didn't go away, but got worse. Finally, surgery and radiation saved her in the nick of time.

My life experience is that problems usually don't go away; they stay as they are or get worse. That's not pessimistic ... it's realistic. I've found I'm always better off acting to solve the problem sooner rather than later.

6. **Others are to blame for the way things are.**

Blaming others gives power away and says: "There's nothing I can do about it. People, events, circumstances are out of my control." It also avoids taking responsibility when we're actually part of the problem.

We can run this belief on past events, too. We can let things from 20 years ago direct our lives, when rationally they have no power.

Blaming others lets our emotions slide into helplessness and depression, or anger at what others are doing ... or did. Either way, we're discouraged and probably do little to change things.

7. That's how I feel, so it must be true.

Most feelings come from what we think and believe. Faulty thinking creates unreliable feelings. If we use these feelings as evidence for the truth, we've left reality behind.

It can work like this:

> I reckon X is the case.
>
> I've got strong feelings about this.
>
> So X is true.

The trap is that X may *not* be the case. We may choose not to check that because we 'know' it is true. But regardless of how strong the feelings are, they are not evidence, and X may *not* be the case.

Our emotions are important guides in the search for reality. But when we reason with our emotions instead of rationally, we'll probably go off course.

Here's the **Top 7 Hit Parade of Irrational Beliefs** again:

1. Life must be fair ... especially to me.

2. If I don't get love, approval and admiration from people, then I'm worthless.

3. When I make a mistake it's awful, terrible and catastrophic.

4. I can't do that.

5. Problems go away when I ignore them.

6. Others are to blame for the way things are.

7. That's how I feel, so it must be true.

You'll notice that these irrational beliefs are all either ...
● deeply pessimistic
  (I can't do that) or ...
● cut off from reality
  (Problems go away when I ignore them)

Damaging, irrational beliefs hit us like this.

Irrational belief

(I can't do that)

leads to ...

⬇

Self-defeating emotion

(Helpless and hopeless fog)

which leads to ...

⬇

Self-defeating behaviour

(Don't even try)

so we get ...

⬇

Negative consequences

(Not much change and growth)

Irrational beliefs cage us in

They can sound so believable when we say them to ourselves. After a while, they become automatic.

> "You can't trust a (woman, man). I know."

> "I couldn't do that in a fit."

> "Let it go for a month or two and see what happens."

> "Those (employees, managers, unions, government) caused it, as usual. There's nothing I can do."

> "I'm hopeless at public speaking. I've got to write it all out before I speak or I freeze up."

We all have automatic beliefs that jump into our self-talk uninvited. They can run for years without being challenged. Some keep us caged like the mouse on the treadmill. We look busy, but we're going nowhere.

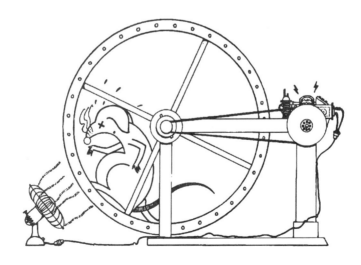

In Chapter 13 you'll find ways to challenge irrational beliefs and turn the treadmill into a ladder. With optimistic self-talk and better grounding in reality, we're more likely to climb the heights of achievement.

No matter what you believe, it doesn't change the facts.
Al Kersha

We are so constituted that we believe the most incredible things; and, once they are engraved upon the memory, woe to him who would endeavour to erase them.
Johann von Goethe

Whatever we believe about ourselves is what we become.
J. Melvin Witmer

Summary so far ...

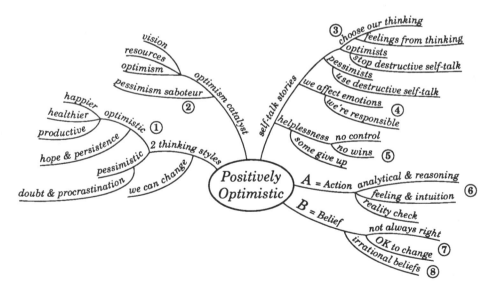

Pause, reflect and apply

We've probably all got some irrational beliefs we love and cherish. Do you recognise some of your favourites?

Chapter 9

Belief ...
Sad and sorry
self-talk stories

The mind is its own place and in itself can make a heaven of hell, a hell of heaven.

John Milton

In Chapter 8 we heard irrational beliefs about life in general. Now let's listen to some common self-talk stories about specific actions and events.

When some action or event happens, we use self-talk to describe and explain it to ourselves. The kind of words we use, and the sort of stories we tell, affect how we feel and act. Our words and stories can be optimistic or pessimistic.

Our self-talk words affect how we feel.

We can use hot, angry words to fan the flames of our feelings so we can't think clearly. We get mad, stay mad and come to enjoy it.

Or, we can use cooler, calmer words to say what we feel and still think clearly. It's our choice, and there will be consequences.

Here are some examples of hot words.

Explosive anger

"I'm absolutely furious!!! He makes me so mad when he does this. I told him to 💣✳💣 ..."

"This is catastrophic. She said she'd ...... and then did nothing. It's a disaster. How are we supposed to get the job done with stupid ✳💣💣 idiots like her in the team?"

"Oh, what a ✳💣✳💣✳! Those 💣✳✳💣 let us down again. I'm going to tell them to 💣💣💣."

When we use swearing and violent language like this, inside or outside our heads, then ZING ... up goes our emotion and out goes rational thinking. That's unlikely to solve problems in the long-term. And it easily pushes us into pessimism.

Catastrophising

Catastrophising is searching for the worst possible explanation and siezing on that.

It's creating awful, horrible, terrible stories about a situation.

It's searching for the worm hiding in the beautiful apple.

Who wouldn't feel miserable after a few hours of that?

This is a favourite pastime for pessimists. It's guaranteed to make you feel miserable, helpless and hopeless. And it opens the door to procrastination, with a bucket of juicy excuses to do nothing about the situation.

Self put-downs

"You ＊ ☼ ＊ fool! You've done it again. You'll *never* learn."

"Any idiot could have done better than you."

"Golly I'm a dill!! She made a complete ass of me over that."

This entertaining habit keeps schoolyard insults echoing through our heads. It's a fast track to pessimism and unhappiness.

Judging and blaming

"He's a ⁂ ⁂! That incompetent fool should have done what I said. Now look. He's ruined everything."

"They couldn't fight their way out of a paper bag. They're hopeless. Everything they do drags us down."

"I told her she musn't stay overnight. She's really done it this time. I'm grounding her for three months."

All our lives we've been told ...

should	must	got to
shouldn't	musn't	ought to
can't	will	oughtn't
couldn't	won't	doesn't
	wouldn't	isn't

Sometimes these words *are* helpful. But they also can be value judgements that we make for other people. When they choose to do otherwise, we're set up for irritation. They can also be negative downers that keep us trapped in doing what we've always done.

Judging, blaming, commanding and controlling are unlikely to solve the problem. And we'll likely damage relationships as we try to take control away from other people.

Judging others and gossiping is a special favourite in Australia, and feeds the tall poppy syndrome. This destructive habit costs Australia heavily. It's based on a scarcity mentality - if you win, I lose. So, rather than celebrate the success of others, it's entertaining to cut them down.

Idolising

"He's fantastic! I could never be like that."

"Oh, I'd love to travel in Europe like she does. It just comes naturally to her. I wouldn't know where to start."

"It's easy for you. I struggle and slave and yet I never get those results."

Of course, some people *do* have more ability than others. But, it's probably 20% natural ability and 80% persistence that wins most success. Idolising tries to excuse us from personal responsibility, and feeds helplessness and pessimism.

Sad and sorry thinking habits

Lots of us hear ourselves saying these words and stories. Here's the list again.

- Explosive anger
- Catastrophising
- Self put-downs
- Judging and blaming
- Idolising

These gems don't do much for us. They can wreck relationships, damage self-esteem, raise emotions that delay solving problems, and send us into pessimism.

In Chapters 10 and 13 you'll find practical ways to create optimistic self-talk stories that leave us more hopeful and energised.

Remember, we choose the way we think most of the time. If we keep using destructive self-talk, we'll suffer the consequences.

It's a habit we can change. If we do, we'll be more effective ...

* on the inside, dealing with our own feelings

* on the outside, dealing with other people's feelings.

Then we can put our energy into meeting challenges rather than angry and self-pitying wheel spinning.

By the way, what do lots of Aussies say when they're asked:

"How are you today?" ... or

"'Ow yer goin', mate?"

They'll use a kind of double negative:

"Not bad"

Or on a spectacular, wonderful, fabulous day ...

"Not too bad" ... or

"Not real bad"

Now that's inspirational! I'd rather say ...

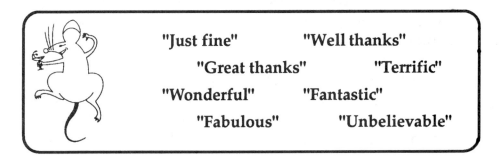

"Just fine"   "Well thanks"

"Great thanks"   "Terrific"

"Wonderful"   "Fantastic"

"Fabulous"   "Unbelievable"

Almost anything is better than ... "Not bad."

Here's an example of how this self-talk works

In this chapter we've heard some common ways of making miserable self-talk stories. To help see how this works in practice, let's try them in a possible life situation.

In the following table you'll find a frustrating sales event described. Most sales people have had an experience like this.

The left hand 'B' column has pessimistic self-talk. The right hand 'B' column has optimistic self-talk about the same situation. As you go through the coming chapters you'll hear how these two streams develop. The comparison will give you a feel for the way these concepts work in practice. Then Chapter 15 gives you some more examples in other fields of life.

The box labelled 'A' describes the action or event. The boxes labelled 'B' are pessimistic or optimistic beliefs about the action.

A You've given your customer good service and regular sales visits for two years. You submit a proposal for an important equipment upgrade. Your customer says they will definitely go with you. But, when you follow up a week later, the customer has bought elsewhere.

Pessimistic track	Optimistic track
B "🔥✳✱🔥 That proves it! Buyers are liars. I'm an idiot for believing them. The same thing happened last week with that mob in Devonport. I get sucked in every time. And, now I'll never make my budget for the quarter. I was relying on that sale. Heck, they said it was mine! What do I have to do?"	**B** "That's so frustrating, after all those sales calls. I'm very unhappy about it. What happened during the sale? Was it the equipment itself, my relationship with the buyer, or perhaps the sales technique? What did I do right? What could I improve? What can I learn from this?"

> Things that are done, it is needless to speak about.
> Things that are past, it is needless to blame.
>   *Confucius*

Summary so far ...

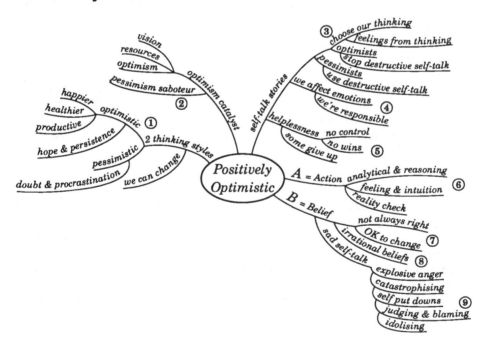

- vision
- resources
- optimism
- pessimism saboteur ②
- optimism catalyst

- happier
- healthier
- productive
- hope & persistence
- doubt & procrastination
- optimistic ①
- pessimistic
- 2 thinking styles
- we can change

Positively Optimistic

- self-talk stories
  - ③ choose our thinking
    - feelings from thinking
    - optimists
    - stop destructive self-talk
    - pessimists
    - use destructive self-talk
  - we affect emotions ④
    - we're responsible
  - helplessness no control
    - no wins
    - some give up ⑤

- A = Action
  - analytical & reasoning
  - feeling & intuition ⑥
  - reality check
  - not always right
  - OK to change ⑦
- B = Belief
  - irrational beliefs ⑧
  - sad self-talk
    - explosive anger
    - catastrophising
    - self put downs
    - judging & blaming ⑨
    - idolising

Pause, reflect and apply

Most people use some of these habits … explosive anger, catastrophising, self put-downs, judging and blaming, idolising. List some of your favourites here.

Chapter 10

Belief ...
Super self-talk
stories

I always tried to turn every disaster into an opportunity.
John D. Rockefeller

So far we've heard how irrational beliefs, and sad and sorry self-talk stories can send us into pessimistic feelings. They hold us back from getting on with solving problems.

Now let's hear how super self-talk stories can help us live happier, healthier and more productive lives ... and attract life's riches.

Saying what we mean while staying in control

When unwanted events happen around us, we can say ...

"We missed the contract. That's frustrating after all the work we put in. I'm disappointed and unhappy about it. Let's review what happened, and look for lessons for next time."

"It's unfortunate that she won't join us. This set-back is inconvenient for our customers and puts our program at risk."

"His unexpected decision puts us at a serious disadvantage. What can we do to keep our idea alive?"

Notice the words here?

frustrating	disappointed	unhappy	
unfortunate	set-back	inconvenient	at risk
unexpected	serious	disadvantage	

These words say what we mean and show our feelings. They are real. Yet they avoid emotional explosions that stop us being effective. We stay on track for doing something positive about our long-term interests. It's an easier recovery to optimism and positive action.

Sometimes 'righteous indignation' *is* in order. Descriptive words like these let it out without making us prisoners of anger that slows our recovery.

Well, we've talked about the words. Now let's look at the stories that we use to explain our experiences to ourselves. They can be optimistic or pessimistic ... it's our choice.

There are three important dimensions in our self-talk stories as we explain what's happening around us. They are:

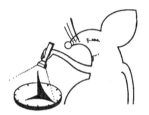

* **Time** – how often is it happening?

* **Place** – where is it happening?

* **Cause** – who's really responsible?

We'll look at each one now.

1. Time

We need to explain: "**How often** does this happen?"

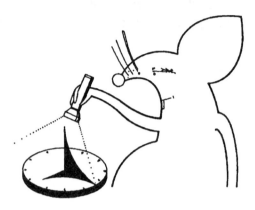

Let's say something frustrates us. We might say ...

"Now that's odd. Generally I have no problem getting it to work. This is unusual." [*optimistic*]

or

"It happened again! It always goes wrong! Every time I try it, I fail. I'll never get it right." [*pessimistic*]

When things **go well** over time ...

*   **optimists** view it as **normal**, and expect nothing else

*   **pessimists** view it as **unusual**, not expected.

When things **go poorly** over time …

- **optimists** view it as **unusual,** not expected

- **pessimists** view it as **normal,** and expect nothing else.

Time

Optimists feel empowered and hopeful.

Pessimists feel helpless and hopeless

… now and in the future.

Reality check

If unwanted events *are* normal, maybe it's time to act and change the situation.

2. Place

We need to explain: "**How widely** does this happen?" **Place** can be a geographic area. Or it can be people like prospective clients, customers, team members, colleagues in organisations, sports club competitors, relatives, friends, and so on.

When something frustrates us, we might say ...

"OK, so it didn't work here with these people, but that doesn't mean it won't work over there. Remember how well I did in ... " [*optimistic*]

or

"It bombed in Adelaide with those people. Now it's failed in Perth too. It won't work anywhere, no matter who I try it with." [*pessimistic*]

When things **go well** with people and places …

    ✳   **optimists** expect it - **everywhere**

    ✳   **pessimists** view it as **exceptional** - just here.

When things **go poorly** with people and places …

    ●   **optimists** view it as **exceptional** - just here

    ●   **pessimists** expect it - **everywhere**.

Place

Optimists feel empowered and hopeful.

Pessimists feel helpless and hopeless

… everywhere, with everybody.

Reality check

If unwanted events *are* happening everywhere with everybody, maybe it's time to act and change the situation.

3. Cause

We need to explain: **"Who caused** this to happen?"

When we're unhappy about something, we might say ...

"Yeah, well. Let's get this straight. They made decisions that wrecked the whole project. I did all anyone could have done to pick up the pieces." [*optimistic*]

   or

"I did it. It's obviously my fault. I messed the whole thing up for everybody. I'm just a failure." [*pessimistic*]

When things **go well** around them ...

*   **optimists** personalise it - **my work**

*   **pessimists** externalise it - **not my work.**

When things **go poorly** around them ...

•   **optimists** externalise it - **not my work**

•   **pessimists** personalise it - **my work.**

Cause

Optimists feel empowered and hopeful.

Pessimists feel helpless and hopeless

... about who makes things happen.

Reality check

If unwanted events *are* your work, maybe it's time to change what you're doing.

Optimists have problems and challenges like everyone else. But their self-talk stories help them act differently from pessimists.

 We can use our self-talk stories to explain events more optimistically.
We can create **super self-talk stories**.

When unwanted events happen, work through …

       * **Time** – how often is it happening?

       * **Place** – where is it happening?

       * **Cause** – who's really responsible?

Remember that **pessimists** tend to …

 generalise

spread

personalise

       … the problem

using **time, place** and **cause** to pessimistically explain what happened.

Whereas **optimists** tend to ...

isolate

limit

externalise

... the problem

using **time**, **place** and **cause** to optimistically explain what happened.

The pessimist's choice is pretty desperate. If we're telling sabotage self-talk stories like ...

"It's always and everywhere my fault."

wrapped up with ...

- explosive anger
- catastrophising
- self put-downs
- judging and blaming
- idolising

then we'll feel ...

helpless, hopeless and useless, and ...

that's a recipe for misery and depression.

Being real

Of course, there's no point in lying to yourself about adversity because ...

* lying is unethical and self-destructive

* it takes us away from reality

* we're less likely to solve the problem, and more likely to hurt others.

We're always better off being real.

The ideas in this chapter work. We can say what we mean without explosive words, and use time, place and cause to explain actions optimistically.

The payoff is huge. Optimistic explanations build faith and hope in ourselves. We can rouse the energy to take action, because we believe we can make a difference.

The ideas can be practiced and learnt, too. You can make them part of your automatic self-talk.

As I've practiced these skills over the years, it's helped me to stop sinking as low when my going gets tough, and to get back up faster. I still feel frustrated and irritated at times. But, these ideas help me work through the feelings faster and get back to hope and action. And that makes for a happier life.

> We must have strong minds, ready to accept the facts as they are …
>
> *Harry Truman*
>
> Consider every mistake you do make as an asset.
>
> *Paul J. Meyer*

Summary so far …

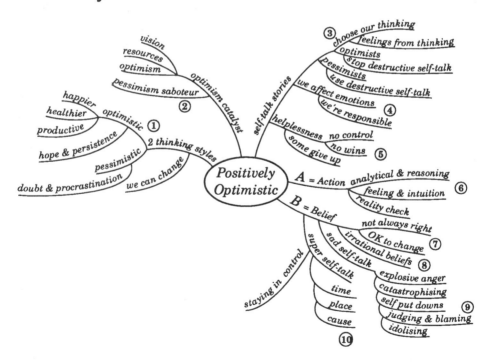

...se, reflect and apply

How's your language when your going gets tough? What changes could you make to take the heat out of your self-talk?

Think back to a recent action that wasn't what you wanted. How did you explain it in time, place and cause?

How could you have explained it differently in time, place and cause to help you stay more hopeful and optimistic?

Chapter 11

Belief ...
Telling our
self-talk stories

Any idea, plan, or purpose may be placed in the mind
through repetition of thought.

Napoleon Hill

You've seen cattle chewing their cud - at least on television. Camels, sheep, goats and giraffes do it too. These animals are called ruminants. They chew the leaves and send them down to the chemical factory, bring them back for another chew, then send them back. It may sound unpleasant to us, but it works for them.

GLIK!

SLURP!

Some folks do the same with their self-talk stories. They ruminate over them. They tell the story in their head, think about it, set their emotions going, then send the story away for a while.

Then they bring it back and repeat the story, maybe add a few bells and whistles, practice it, repeat, practice, repeat ... then send it away for a while.

Pretty soon they know the script word perfect, repeat it and get the same emotional blast time after time. This can go on for hours, days, months. It's called ...

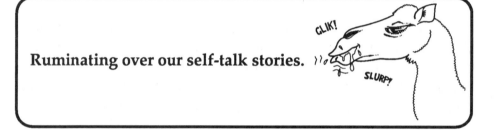

Ruminating over our self-talk stories. CLIK! SLURP!

Sometimes we get excited and go on a crusade with our self-talk stories, telling friends, acquaintances, anyone who'll listen. They all hear the same story, word perfect, as we try to convince them that our story is *the* story.

Well, ruminating is bound to have an effect on our mind. It can be helpful or harmful to us.

Some people use ruminating to their advantage. It goes like this.

Optimistic self-talk stories + ruminating

help us

feel hopeful

so we

 ➡ ➡ ➡ **take action**

This is the idea behind **affirmations** - words, stories or pictures that are revisited frequently to help us ...

❋ replace a current belief that's not helping us

❋ focus on a current belief that is helping us.

Affirmations can be things like …

* poems or lines which you replay in your mind

* pictures of dream boats on the wall

* photos of fabulous holiday resorts in your daily planner

* desk plaques with optimistic messages

… and so on.

The idea is to ruminate and dream about the affirmations as though they are already real. It works well if you're not pushing back with doubts, disbelief and rejecting success.

Affirmations help us think about what we _do_ want, and go after it.

They help us stop thinking about what we _don't_ want, and getting mad about that.

Other people get stuck in pessimistic ruminating. This can lead to a bad case of misplaced importance ... investing time, 'brain space' and emotion on the wrong stuff. It goes like this.

Pessimistic self-talk stories + ruminating

make us

feel hopeless

so we

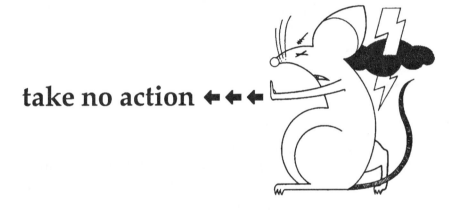

take no action ← ← ←

This is a fast track to depression. If we keep this stuff going on and on, we may need professional help to get out of it.

Pessimistic ruminating is like the self-destructive behaviour of processionary caterpillars when things go wrong.

One processionary caterpillar will start walking and others fall in behind, nose to tail, forming a tight, unbroken line of marching caterpillars. All the decisions in the search for food are left to the leader. The others follow automatically without questioning the outcome.

French naturalist Jean-Henri Fabre got a leader to start circling the lip of a flower pot. As the others fell in close behind, the leader came around and joined up with the rear of the last caterpillar, forming an unbroken chain of followers. None of them was making a decision.

The relentless marching and searching went on for several days and nights. Finally, they fell off the pot from exhaustion and starvation.

This reminds me of ruminating. In nature, when there is a clear leader telling a good story, they all get to the food. Rather like positive affirmations leading us to achievement and fulfillment.

But when the story gets lost or confused, mindless activity takes the place of achievement. Rather like pessimistic ruminating, the outcome is frustrating and self-destructive.

If we find ourselves going around and around in fruitless ruminating, maybe it's time to challenge the direction, and change the outcome.

Most of the time, in ordinary living, we can stop fruitless ruminating by ourselves. We'll talk about the 'how' in Chapter 13.

Any idea, plan, or purpose may be placed in the mind through repetition of thought.

Napoleon Hill

Repeat anything often enough and it will start to become you.

Tom Hopkins

Summary so far ...

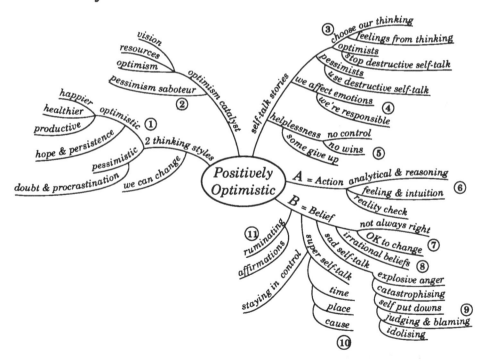

Pause, reflect and apply

Do you hear yourself ruminating over pessimistic self-talk stories? How do you feel when a miserable story is running around and around your head?

Do you use affirmations to shift your thinking and feelings? If so, what works best for you?

Chapter 12

C = Consequence

A = Action

B = Belief

 C = Consequence

D = Dispute

E = Energise

Sooner or later, everyone sits down to a banquet of consequences.

Robert Louis Stevenson

You'll remember that in Chapter 3 we said ...

1. **We choose the way we think most of the time.**

2 **Most feelings come from what we think.**

3. **So, we choose how we feel most of the time.**

Self-talk creates feelings. The self-talk has consequences because our feelings affect whether or not we act.

It goes like this ... ABC.

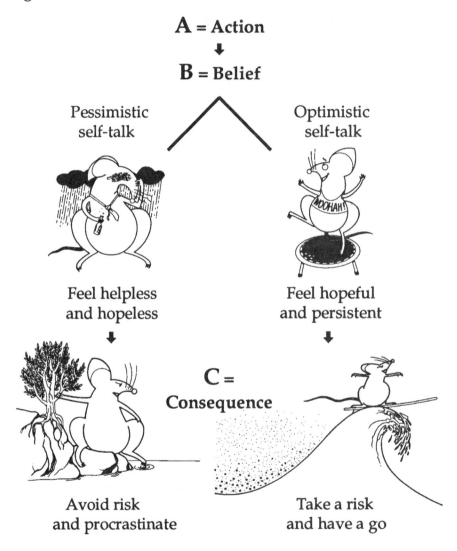

A = Action

B = Belief

Pessimistic self-talk

Optimistic self-talk

Feel helpless and hopeless

Feel hopeful and persistent

C =
Consequence

Avoid risk and procrastinate

Take a risk and have a go

Sometimes we can't do much about the action part of the ABC. People and events which we don't control affect our lives.

But we are always choosing how we think about ourselves and actions around us ... the B = Belief. Our choice of beliefs and attitudes always have consequences ... the C = Consequence. The sum of our lives is the sum of the consequences of countless beliefs and attitudes, lived moment by moment.

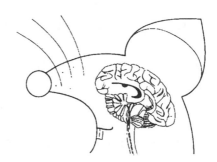

Imagine for a moment a ship sailing from Sydney to Vancouver. A course change of one degree early in the voyage would have an enormous effect after sailing thousands of kilometers. The vessel may reach land in California or Alaska instead.

We saw in Chapter 1 that optimistic thinking has consequences that affect our lives for good. As with the ship on its voyage, small changes in thinking habits will have an enormous cumulative effect over our lifetime.

Simple changes from:

"I can't get that job."   to   "I'll apply and try."

"S/he won't like me."   to   "Would you like a coffee?"

"I'm a school drop-out." to   "I'm starting a part-time class."

... could result in a new career, a new partner and expanded horizons, with decades of difference.

It's Sunday afternoon in Kowloon, Hong Kong. The shopping mall is crowded with families, friends and lovers, looking at each other and the shop windows.

I hear a shriek of excitement up ahead. A three-year old Indian boy is racing towards me, his colourfully dressed mother in hot pursuit.

Suddenly he sees a wall of legs ahead and does a sharp left turn into a clothing shop. With dismay he sees the walls closing in, but straight ahead is an escape. Another loud shriek and he surges forward, his arms and legs flailing.

But, he fails to notice a little boy running fast towards him – and it's himself! Bang into the mirror, long scream and wailing.

The shocked sales assistants gasp and rock back on their heels. Mother rushes in, swoops him up and kisses the bruised nose and wet cheeks.

Sometimes we lose face too, when we meet head-on the consequences of our beliefs and actions. Friends and loved ones shake their heads, having seen it coming.

The ideas in the next chapter can help us change our beliefs and obtain the outcomes we desire.

Now, let's add the consequences to the sales story. The optimistic or pessimistic beliefs lead to very different consequences.

A You've given your customer good service and regular sales visits for two years. You submit a proposal for an important equipment upgrade. Your customer says they will definitely go with you. But, when you follow up a week later, the customer has bought elsewhere.	
Pessimistic track	**Optimistic track**
B "⚡✳✱⚡ That proves it! Buyers are liars. I'm an idiot for believing them. The same thing happened last week with that mob in Devonport. I get sucked in every time. And, now I'll never make my budget for the quarter. I was relying on that sale. Heck, they said it was mine! What do I have to do?"	**B** "That's so frustrating, after all those sales calls. I'm very unhappy about it. What happened during the sale? Was it the equipment itself, my relationship with the buyer, or perhaps the sales technique? What did I do right? What could I improve? What can I learn from this?"
C The infuriated seller takes days to recover. The miserable story gets repeated through the sales and office people, poisoning the atmosphere for everyone.	**C** The disappointed seller feels stung temporarily, but gets going again the next morning. The focus is on gathering evidence and solving the problem for the future. It's a learning experience.

> You are free to do whatever you like. You need only face the consequences.
>
> *Sheldon Kopp*
>
> Who you are is not a discovery but a decision.
>
> *Emma Pierce*

Summary so far ...

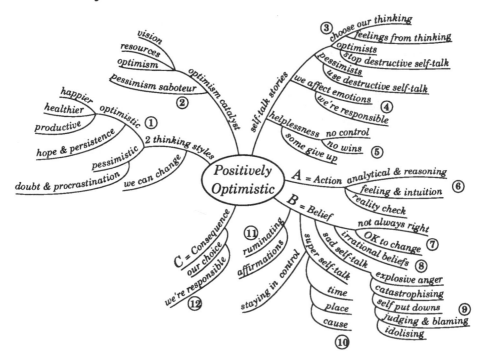

Pause, reflect and apply

What consequences have you seen amongst your friends and acquaintances from …

Optimistic beliefs and self-talk stories

Pessimistic beliefs and self-talk stories.

Positively Optimistic

Chapter 13

D = Dispute

A = Action

B = Belief

C = Consequence

☞ D = Dispute

E = Energise

Change your thoughts and you change your world.
Norman Vincent Peale

People can believe just about anything.

Take the Aztecs, for example. They reckoned they could change the weather, and stop bugs and rot from destroying their crops. How? By cutting people's hearts out on sacrificial altars.

"Oh yeah, but we're smarter than that!" you might say. Maybe so, but the political and environmental events of the 20th century suggest otherwise. The ideas have been different, but just as wild.

A chilling feature of the Nazi murder factories was that the people doing the killing were mostly ordinary people quite like us. Hopefully our beliefs will never involve us in destructive acts. But, each of us can benefit by disputing our beliefs when they obviously aren't working for us - or others.

In Chapter 2 we saw that pushing harder with a stunning vision, perfectly written goals, motivational arm waving, etc doesn't help if we're blocking our progress with pessimistic views.

➡ ➡ ➡ ➡ ➡
Optimistic
effort

⬅ ⬅ ⬅ ⬅ ⬅
Pessimistic
sabotage

Pushing harder and harder   ... sabotage and obstruction
doesn't help if ...   just push back harder

So, the best way to move ahead is ... remove the obstruction. Then all the optimistic beliefs can work for us.

This chapter shows you four effective steps for shifting thinking. They can help you remove sabotage and obstruction ... temporarily and more permanently. Look in the box opposite to see where we're going. Then we'll go through each step in detail.

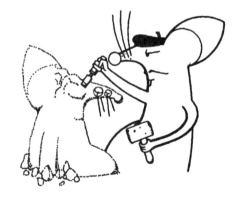

4 steps for shifting thinking

1. Develop awareness

Hear and recognise damaging
beliefs and self-talk while it's happening.

↓

2. Distract yourself from rotten ruminating

Stop pessimistic self-talk
and ruminating.

↓

3. Dispute your self-talk soapies

Challenge assumptions and beliefs.

↓

4. Drive a new self-talk story

Make different explanations;
practice and repeat the new beliefs.

1. Develop awareness

The first step in shifting thinking is to develop awareness of our current self-talk.

Watch the current episodes in your self-talk soapies. Listen for the telltale scenes that push the pessimism story line.

Check the Top 7 Hit Parade of Irrational Beliefs

Listen for your automatic irrational beliefs that lead to self-defeating behaviour.

Check for sad and sorry self-talk stories

Be aware if your self-talk is running a program saying ...

"It's always and everywhere my fault."

wrapped up with ...

- explosive anger
- catastrophising
- self put-downs
- judging and blaming
- idolising

When we hear pessimistic stuff in the script, it's time to hire a new writer. We need to weaken this miserable thinking and change it.

2. Distract yourself from rotten ruminating

Take action to distract yourself from ruminating with awfulising, horrib-lising, catastrophising, pessimistic self-talk.

Distracting gives us a temporary break so we can intervene with our rational mind. Here are effective ways to take time out from the situation:

* slap the wall, shout **"STOP!"** and change what you're doing
* go out for a brisk walk
* go shopping
* do some gardening
* watch a funny movie
* have a sleep
* work out at the gym with aerobic exercise or weights
* read an uplifting and inspiring book
* go out for a swift bike ride
* plan an exciting holiday
* eat out at a favourite restaurant.

    Now we've stopped the self-talk, we can move to change it.

3. Dispute your self-talk soapies

Our self-talk is often a single, persistent voice that rattles on unchallenged. A corrosive monologue that eats away at hope and persistence.

Start a dialogue with a second self-talk voice. Create an 'unreasonable friend' who disputes the automatic self-talk with tough questions. Here are four that help us counsel ourselves.

Any evidence?

"OK, so who says this is true? Where's the evidence?"

Just because we say something to ourselves doesn't make it true. Challenge the script by asking yourself: "Is there any evidence for what I'm saying about this? Is there a better view of (**time, place** and **cause**)?"

For example, when our inner critic says: "You're hopeless!", we believe the voice. But if someone else said the same words we'd probably fight back and defend ourselves. So, defend yourself against destructive self-talk by disputing and demanding evidence. Fight the awfulising and catastrophising.

Any alternatives?

"Yeah well, that's one explanation.   What else have we got?"

Be open minded and search for alternatives. Watch out for: "That's how I feel, so it must be true."

We're often quick to catastrophise, judge and blame ourselves and others. But there may be other explanations which we know nothing about.

For example, we damage relationships when we catastrophise another person's motives and feelings, then act on that belief. Ugh! How many times are we totally wrong!

Does it matter?

When we feel anxiety and emotion rising, it's helpful to ask ourselves: "Well, so what. Does it really matter? Maybe this is misplaced importance at work? Why am I upsetting myself about this?"

And if it is important: "What's the worst thing that can happen, and how do I handle that?"

There's no better tutor for handling adversity than experience. Every lesson learnt adds steel to our spine. We need fear it no more. Past is past.

Does it help?

"Is believing this stuff actually doing me any good? I've got to stop this nonsense and get on with living - right now."

Many of our self-talk stories plainly don't do us any good. We can dispute them, stop them and start again. Self-destructive beliefs and behaviours are the ultimate sabotage.

Sometimes we find it hard to step back, disengage from hot emotion and long-held beliefs. We may not *want* to dispute beliefs which bring satisfaction ... even though it's self-destructive.

Seek help from a trusted friend, peer, coach, mentor. They may confront and dispute your beliefs better than you can. A few straight words from a trusted person can short-circuit a seemingly endless loop of self-destructive ruminating.

For years I feared making telephone 'cold calls' for my business. Good friends confronted my irrational beliefs like ...

> "I can't do that."
>
> "They don't like me."
>
> "I'll irritate them and they'll want to get rid of me."
>
> "I hate doing it."

Their confronting helped me dispute my assumptions. As my beliefs changed, so did my emotions and my voice on the phone. Up went the results, down went the fear.

Get in early

It's well known that negative self-talk, which causes miserable emotions, is nearly always unreliable*. We're better off without this stuff in our lives.

The best time to stop a miserable self-talk story is early, before it gets a life of its own. Jump in early before you start ruminating and pumping up miserable emotion. Distract and dispute before it seems too hard to stop.

*Dr Melvin Witmer, *Pathways to Personal Growth*, 1985

4. Drive a new self-talk story

Here again is the quote from Dr Denis Waitley in Chapter 3:

"Relentless, repetitive self-talk
is what changes our self-image."

Now that we've distracted and disputed, we need to drive a new self-talk story and repeat it to change our self-image. Here's an effective technique to drive new self-talk stories.

What self-talk do I want to change?

Make a list of your awfulising, catastrophising, sabotaging self-talk that you'd like to change. Check for irrational ideas, and sad and sorry self-talk stories that keep running in your head.

If you can't think of any, imagine what you were thinking when something went wrong for you during the last year. What was your self-talk then?

Write down three to five pessimistic self-talk stories that you want to change first. Work on them so you get confidence in the technique.

When these self-talk stories are running in your head:
● How do you feel?
● What images do you have of yourself at home, work, socially?
● What tone of voice is the self-talk?

Write a new script

Now take your three to five miserable self-talk lines one at a time. Write down optimistic lines that mean the opposite of the miserable stuff. Look for encouraging ideas that support your growth and development.

Here are some examples.

Pessimistic: "I never finish anything that I start."
Optimistic: "I excel in everything I begin. I am a finisher."

Pessimistic: "Our customers are a pain in the neck."
Optimistic: "Most of our customers are enjoyable people. I succeed with them."

Pessimistic: "Everyone thinks I'm stupid when I make a mistake."
Optimistic: "I take action and make decisions. Sometimes I make mistakes, and I learn from that."

Pessimistic: "I hate prospecting with people I don't know."
Optimistic: "I know my sales success ratios. Some of my prospects will become customers and friends."

Imagine someone who is running these optimistic stories in their head:

● How would they feel?
● What images would they have of themselves at home, work, socially?
● How would their self-talk sound?

Now you've got two lines you can run. The old, automatic self-destructive stuff, and the new optimistic line. Consequences flow from each one. The next step is to knowingly drive the optimistic line and change your life.

Change the program

Richard Bandler, cofounder of neurolinguistic programming, developed a technique to help us change the program*. Michael McCarthy adapted it**. You'll find the technique set out on the next page.

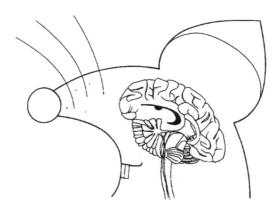

*Richard Bandler, *Using Your Brain - for a Change*, 1985
**Michael McCarthy, *Mastering the Information Age*, 1991

Change the program

1.   Think about one of your miserable self-talk lines, together with its associated feelings and images. Be vividly aware of your emotional state. Hold this in your mind.

2.   Say firmly to yourself: "I am going to change this belief."

3.   Now imagine, way off in the distance, how you will look, sound and feel with the new, opposite belief.

4.   Let the miserable self-talk line get weaker in your mind, and bring the optimistic image closer.

5.   Suddenly, drop the miserable self-talk line and focus totally on the optimistic belief. Change the way you're sitting or standing to act the new part. Be this new person.

6.   Immerse yourself in the feelings, appearance and sounds of this new belief. Imagine you are this person, and what impact it will have on your life.

7.   Go back through steps 1 to 6 a couple more times, with a brief break between each series. You'll notice that the new belief becomes stronger each time.

8.   Then immediately take action that reflects your new belief. See Chapter 14.

Run the new program ... again and again

Some of these miserable self-talk stories have been running for years. They jump into our monologue self-talk uninvited. It's unrealistic to expect them to quit straight away.

You'll remember our vacationing friend from Chapter 11. We talked about affirmations. They can help us replace a current belief that's not helping us, or focus on a current belief that is helping us.

Affirmations are a great example of driving a new self-talk story.

The idea is to run the new program over and over. Three, five, many times each day, until the optimistic line is locked into our self-talk.

Write the optimistic stories down and visit them at regular times throughout the day. Feel, see and hear the new ideas as part of you. Spend the time to immerse yourself in the optimistic ideas.

It makes sense. After all, we ruminate over our awfulising self-talk heaps of times ... around and around and around. Our mind and body react like it's real, actually happening. Pumped up emotion. Stalled progress.

Good stuff works just as well ... for us, instead of against us.

Reality check

We'd better do a reality check when we write our affirmations.

Our affirmations need to fit the realistic expectations of our existence. There's no point in creating new self-talk that keeps us from reality again. We're no better off.

Perhaps we have a 10 year goal that requires a lot of growth from us. Telling ourselves we're already there makes little sense.

It does make sense to climb one step at a time, while keeping the end in mind. Affirmations can help us make the small changes that add up to success.

Let's review D = Dispute

Here's how the steps tie together.

1. Develop awareness

Hear and recognise damaging beliefs
and self-talk while it's happening.

↓

2. Distract yourself from rotten ruminating

Stop pessimistic self-talk
and ruminating.

↓

3. Dispute your self-talk soapies

Challenge assumptions and beliefs.

↓

4. Drive a new self-talk story

Make different explanations;
practice and repeat the new beliefs.

This is beautiful stuff!
It can help change your life.

———— ✻ ————

Some years ago an event took place that I didn't like. Really didn't like. My emotions seemed out of control. It seemed like a black bear would come rumbling out of the forest and take over my head, any time it wanted. And then the ruminating would start. Around and around. I couldn't keep the bear away, because I didn't know about distracting and disputing.

Now the bear is back in the forest. I'm in control, most of the time. Haven't seen the bear in years. Why? Because when things go wrong as they sometimes will, a new self-talk switches on:

"Settle down, pal. You've got a view about this matter, but almost no facts. Let's talk to the people involved and get some information. There could be many reasons for their actions. Don't get yourself upset about it. Remember, you didn't set up this situation, they did. And, don't forget the excellent relationships with their offices in other States over the last two years. This problem is most unusual. You're good at this, and you'll solve it."

———— ✻ ————

You can learn and practice the thinking skills in these chapters to change your life too, and the lives of those around you.

Here's an example Dispute story for the pessimistic side. There's no need to dispute the optimistic side, since we're working to achieve an optimistic view.

A You've given your customer good service and regular sales visits for two years. You submit a proposal for an important equipment upgrade. Your customer says they will definitely go with you. But, when you follow up a week later, the customer has bought elsewhere.

Pessimistic track	Optimistic track
B "※☀✷※ That proves it! Buyers are liars. I'm an idiot for believing them. The same thing happened last week with that mob in Devonport. I get sucked in every time. And, now I'll never make my budget for the quarter. I was relying on that sale. Heck, they said it was mine! What do I have to do?"	**B** "That's so frustrating, after all those sales calls. I'm very unhappy about it. What happened during the sale? Was it the equipment itself, my relationship with the buyer, or perhaps the sales technique? What did I do right? What could I improve? What can I learn from this?"
C The infuriated seller takes days to recover. The miserable story gets repeated through the sales and office people, poisoning the atmosphere for everyone.	**C** The disappointed seller feels stung temporarily, but gets going again the next morning. The focus is on gathering evidence and solving the problem for the future. It's a learning experience.
D "Let's ask the customer how the decision was made to buy from our competition. Perhaps our product or price is suddenly not competitive. Maybe that also explains the Devonport loss. Anyway, settle down. Our company doesn't have 100% of the market. These disappointments are going to happen more often than not. Let's look at trends and the big picture over six months, not just individual cases."	

Reprogramming the unconscious beliefs that block fuller awareness of our creative/intuitive capabilities depends upon a key characteristic of the mind, namely that it responds to what is vividly imagined as though it were real experience.

Willis Harman

Acceptance of what has happened is the first step to overcoming the consequences of any misfortune.

William James

Summary so far ...

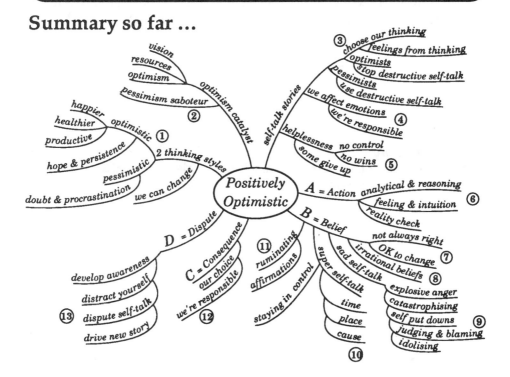

Pause, reflect and apply

Distract

What are your favourite ways to distract your rotten ruminating?

Dispute

Think back to an event which didn't work out well for you, and you felt pretty hurt. How could you have disputed your self-talk and worked through it with a better outcome and less painful emotion?

Drive a new story

Write down the top three miserable self-talk stories you want to change. How could you re-script them as optimistic and helpful self-talk?

Chapter 14

E = Energise

A = Action

B = Belief

C = Consequence

D = Dispute

☞ **E = Energise**

All that is necessary to break the spell of inertia and frustration is this: act as if it were impossible to fail.

Dorothea Brande

The pessimist's problem

If we want to live a happier, healthier and more productive life, we have to take risks and keep changing. That's a problem for pessimistic thinkers who avoid risk and change. They get stuck in helplessness, indifference and fear.

Helplessness   If we believe that:

"It's always and everywhere my fault."

"Nothing I do makes any difference."

… then we'll likely feel helpless, give up and take no action.

Indifference If we believe that:
   "I don't care about it, so why should I make an effort?"
... then we've opened the door wide to procrastination.
   Elie Wiesel, a survivor of Nazi concentration camps, put it this way:

> The opposite of love is not hatred,
> The opposite of hope is not despair,
> The opposite of mental health is not madness,
> The opposite of remembering is not forgetting,
> In every case the opposite is nothing but indifference.*

Fear   If we believe that:
   "I'll get zapped if I have a go at that."
   "What would everyone think if I failed?"
... we'll freeze up and do nothing.

   All three beliefs - helplessness, indifference and fear - lead to pessimism and inaction. So, if we want to shift our thinking towards optimism, what can we do?

Dispute our pessimistic beliefs

and

Energise - take action

* As quoted by Charles Birch, *Feelings*, 1995

Stop fence sitting with helplessness, indifference and fear …

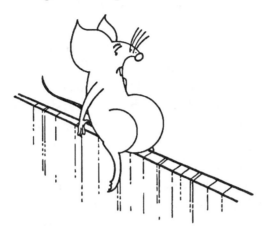

… and energise ourselves to persistent, constructive action. Nothing else works over the long-term.

High quality, optimistic self-talk is not enough by itself. We must take action. Sometimes that means *making* ourselves do courageous acts. Soon we become accustomed to this new operating level and it gets easier. Later, as we enjoy this new competence, we wonder why we found it so worrisome before.

An Australian hero of the II World War was an inspiring example of triumph against helplessness, indifference and fear.

In 1939, Sir Edward 'Weary' Dunlop joined the Australian 2nd AIF in Palestine as a captain in the medical corps. He served in Libya, was swept up in the retreat through Greece and Crete, and joined the Rats of Tobruk before the 7th Division left for Australia.

During the journey south, the troops were diverted to Java in a desperate effort to halt the Japanese advance towards Australia. Sir Edward was captured by the Japanese in February 1942. As a lieutenant colonel and Japanese prisoner, he was appointed commander of the Allied General Hospital in Batavia, Java. He and other doctors battled cholera, beri-beri, jungle ulcers, malaria and malnutrition with an almost total lack of medicines, and using instruments made from knives, forks and bamboo shoots.

Sir Edward was among 22,000 Australians captured in Malaya and Singapore, over 7,000 of whom died amongst the brutality and savagery of the Japanese military. Sir Edward served his fellow POWs on the notorious Burma-Thailand railway, where so many died as forced labourers.

In this appallingly brutal environment, 'Weary' Dunlop rejected helplessness, indifference and fear. Fellow POW and former Australian Federal Minister Tom Uren said of him: "He was the tallest tree in the forest. He was a light and a beacon of hope in those dark days of 1943 and 44 ... might I speak to our young Australians about this beautiful, skilled, courageous person."*

After six years of war, Sir Edward Dunlop's optimism never failed him. He contributed widely to the Australian and international community until his death in 1993, aged 85 years.

* As quoted by Shirley McLaughlin, *The Driving Force*, 1995

So, how can we reject helplessness, indifference and fear?

> # Do what you know must be done (logic)
> ## even though
> # you don't want to. (feelings)
>
> # Just do it!

Successful people do this. Pretty soon you get through the fear and your feelings improve. It's that simple. And, it's all driven by self-talk.

How do you get started?

> ## Dispute pessimistic beliefs
> ### and
> ### take action

A You've given your customer good service and regular sales visits for two years. You submit a proposal for an important equipment upgrade. Your customer says they will definitely go with you. But, when you follow up a week later, the customer has bought elsewhere.

Pessimistic track	Optimistic track
B "❋✳❋✳ That proves it! Buyers are liars. I'm an idiot for believing them. The same thing happened last week with that mob in Devonport. I get sucked in every time. And, now I'll never make my budget for the quarter. I was relying on that sale. Heck, they said it was mine! What do I have to do?"	**B** "That's so frustrating, after all those sales calls. I'm very unhappy about it. What happened during the sale? Was it the equipment itself, my relationship with the buyer, or perhaps the sales technique? What did I do right? What could I improve? What can I learn from this?"
C The infuriated seller takes days to recover. The miserable story gets repeated through the sales and office people, poisoning the atmosphere for everyone.	**C** The disappointed seller feels stung temporarily, but gets going again the next morning. The focus is on gathering evidence and solving the problem for the future. It's a learning experience.

D "Let's ask the customer how the decision was made to buy from our competition. Perhaps our product or price is suddenly not competitive. Maybe that also explains the Devonport loss. Anyway, settle down. Our company doesn't have 100% of the market. These disappointments are going to happen more often than not. Let's look at trends and the big picture over six months, not just individual cases."

Here's the last step - take action to solve the problem.

In Chapter 15 you'll find more examples, from sport, family, teams and study.

E The salesperson gets going to fill the pipeline with more and more prospects. Then when individual cases are unsuccessful, it's not such a worry.

It is always your next move.

Napoleon Hill

There are no gains without pains.

Benjamin Franklin

All things are difficult before they are easy.

Thomas Fuller

Do what you fear and fear disappears.

David Joseph Schwartz

To make anything a habit, do it;
to not make it a habit, do not do it;
to unmake a habit, do something else in place of it.

Epictetus

Sow an action and you reap a habit;
sow a habit and you reap a character;
sow a character and you reap a destiny.

William James

Summary of the whole ABCDE ...

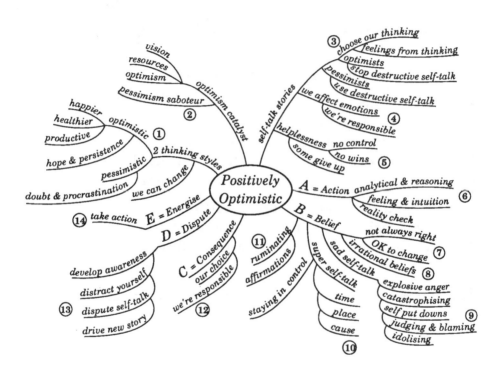

Pause, reflect and apply

Think of a situation that's challenging you now. What can you do to dispute and energise so you move ahead to a solution?

Positively Optimistic

Chapter 15

Hear and feel how it works

So far we've talked about ...

Why we're better off with optimistic thinking; and

What works in shifting our thinking.

Now let's hear **how** optimistic thinking works in the ABCDE model.

Here are some examples from personal, business and sport situations. Of course, the situations aren't exactly like your experiences, but you can draw out the principles.

You'll see the contrast between optimistic and pessimistic self-talk stories. That's a great way to learn how it works.

A World Champion Michael Doohan passed team mate Alex Criville on the last corner during the 1996 500cc motorcycle Spanish Grand Prix. Criville had led for most of the race in front of his home crowd. In a desperate effort to regain the lead, Criville over accelerated and crashed heavily. Criville stood up in time to see Doohan take the chequered flag. Doohan didn't know that Criville had crashed.

Pessimistic track	Optimistic track
B "That stinks!! The crowd upset me and let Mick close in. I want the result declared on the preceding lap. That was my win, after all I did. Anyone can see I should get first place. ✸ ☀ ☀ ✸ What do I have to do to beat Mick? He does this stuff every time. Remember at ... "	**B** "I thought I had it in my hand. Mick was obviously waiting for that corner. Next time I'll have to shut him out tighter. Hey, this is the best season ever for me. Nobody else is challenging Mick like I am. Well, my body's OK. The bike performed brilliantly. Next week!"
C He stews over it for days and the relationship with Mick, his teammate in the Honda camp, gets tense. All that judging and blaming doesn't change the result, but keeps the anger going strong.	**C** He feels frustrated and disappointed after riding so well. But he knows Mick is the best in the world, and the gap is closing. So, back on the bike and out for more practice. It's a long season.

D "Mick's good. Really good. But, I held him off for 24 laps. What an achievement. No-one else in the world is as good as us. And Mick's race craft is brilliant. I'm learning all the time. By the end of the season I'll be ready to challenge hard in '97. I can beat him at ... and maybe at ... where the track suits me. Just watch and learn. And keep the door closed so he can't do that again."

PS. Criville did protest, but Honda ordered the protest withdrawn. He recovered from this loss and won a later race in the season from Mick by 2,000ths of a second - the width of the front tyre!

E Study the video of the last corner and see how Mick did it. Watch his style and learn to think like him, so as to anticipate where he'll strike. Ride hard.

Sport

A "Paul turned 16 a couple of months ago. We've always had a close family and the older kids went through just fine. But Paul took off with a couple of mates and we've had no contact for three weeks. We're not sure where he is, although the mother of one of his group thinks they went fruit picking at Batlow."

Pessimistic track	Optimistic track
B "What a little 🐀 🐀 🐀 🐀 . After all we've done for him. He's got no right to treat us this way. Just wait 'til we get our hands on him. That's if he ever comes back. I bet he's on drugs already and sleeping around. Good grief. Where did we go wrong? And now Suzie is 14. She'll be next! I wish we'd ..."	**B** We feel concerned and frustrated. "Where is the boy? Is he OK? Well, we've given him our very best and all the love we've got. He's a good kid inside. The others have all grown up well. He will too. We'll give him our love and support when he calls. We can let him be himself, his way."
C Mum and Dad are just about paralysed. They can't think of anything but the disasters Paul is no doubt getting into. They feel shattered and helpless.	**C** The sick feeling in the stomach is still with Mum and Dad, but it's not crippling. They're able to think about other things. It's the waiting that bites. But, they can get on with living.

D "Well, he's gone off with his mates. At least he's not alone or without support, and they're pretty good kids. We think it's not helpful for him, but lots of other kids have done this and turned out fine. He chose this - it's not our fault. The older ones were pretty stable. Paul's got a good head on his shoulders. He knows what's right. Let's keep the door open. We can talk to him about letting us know what he's doing ..."

Family

E Talk to the other parents and keep the support network going. Stop ruminating over catastrophising self-talk. Have faith in your 16 years of parenting.

A Your team is manufacturing A4 size binders for sale in retail stationery stores. Quality and timeliness are vital. There's no room for error in a competitive market. Your team is on a performance bonus plan where you win or lose together. Josie has been erratic for a week - late to work, a day off, poor concentration. She's a key player and the team performance is off the pace. Your bonus is threatened.

Pessimistic track	Optimistic track
B "That ✳✳ 💢 Josie is ruining our production again. She's wrecked our speed and quality all week. What an idiot. I can't afford to lose a single dollar of that bonus. I'm going to tell her to shape up or ship out. She's messing up my profits. It'll take days to get back into our high speed routine."	**B** "I wonder what's happening with Josie. This is very unusual. She's been a terrific team player for two years. And, she worked in another successful team before joining us. I can't believe she's doing this deliberately. Something must be upsetting her pretty badly. Let's act quickly to see how we can help her."
C Josie gets a broadside of abuse. Whatever chance of helping her is lost as she retreats into herself. Trust is damaged and Josie feels helpless to cope with family and work troubles.	**C** The team relies on their trust and open communication to support Josie through urgent family troubles. They do more cross training so they can cover for each other better in emergencies.

D "Stop ruminating over this stuff. You don't have a clue what's actually happening around Josie. You know she needs the bonus as much as you do. Something big must be troubling her. There's no way that she's just dropped her bundle on the team. She's never done that before. Actually, she's always encouraged everyone else. Stop judging her when you don't know the facts. Abusing her isn't going to help."

E A team member close to Josie talks quietly to her about her situation. The team acts to share the load and solve the problem quickly so everyone benefits.

A This is it. The last term to finish your study program. You've done well so far, but this subject has been a trial. You've not enjoyed the classes, and the instructor seemed distant towards you. It's been a struggle to hang on. If you don't pass this exam, you've got to wait a year to have another go at it. So, the pressure is on.

Pessimistic track	Optimistic track
B "I've had it. This is a disaster. I'm an idiot for blowing it in the last term. I'll never be able to finish the program now. And the company will probably tell me to leave. ✳ ⚲ ⚲ ✳ If only I was like Julie. She does it so easily. ⚲ ⚲ And that idiot instructor …"	**B** "I'm OK with this exam. Look at my track record. I get better each term as I gain experience with the whole program. This will be the same. Anyway, I've done all the homework, read all the assignments and been to every class. I've done the preparation like I always do. And I'll do well like I always do."
C You're a bundle of nerves. What you do know gets lost in an emotional freeze. You sit there for an hour, unable to think and too ashamed to get up and leave before some others do.	**C** You do well because you're able to concentrate. Your hope and faith in your own ability let you cope with the normal and healthy tension.

D "Hey, wait a minute. You haven't even seen the exam yet. Sure you've had some challenges in this subject, but you've done all you can throughout the term. And, you've passed everything else in the course. You've done it before, and you can do it now. Stop catastrophising and focus on better preparation. Anyway, what if you don't pass? No-one else has been sacked for that. You won't be either."

Study

E Go back over your summaries and assignments. Keep working at it, especially the bits you're unsure of. Fix up your weak areas. Practice, rehearse …

Positively Optimistic

Chapter 16

You can spread infectious optimism

It is good to have an end to journey towards, but it is the journey that matters in the end.

Ursula Le Guin

Most of us find changing ourselves to be challenging, slow and plain hard work. Big changes are hard to sustain more than a few days, and we slip back to old patterns. So it's probably unrealistic to try and suddenly become a lot more optimistic all the time.

My successes have come in taking small steps, one at a time. Steps that individually make small demands on me, but taken together over time have added meaning, interest and fulfillment to my journey.

I invite you to review the techniques in this book and patiently, persistently practice the skills of optimism. Make small increments of change, steadily building new patterns of thought. Major changes in life often start from seemingly small events. We can dramatically change our lives by listening to, and changing our self-talk about the common, every day, small things.

To help you on your way, here's a summary of the big ideas in A = Action through to E = Energise. Then the rest of the chapter suggests ways you can spread infectious optimism.

A = Action

Analysing and reasoning

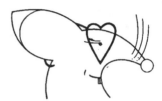

Feeling and intuition

Reality check

B = Belief

My view is one view.
There could be a better view.
It's OK to change my view.

The Top 7 Hit Parade of Irrational Beliefs

1. Life must be fair ... especially for me.
2. If I don't get love, approval and admiration from people, then I'm worthless.
3. When I make a mistake it's awful, terrible and catastrophic.
4. I can't do that.
5. Problems go away when I ignore them.
6. Others are to blame for the ways things are.
7. That's how I feel, so it must be true.

Sad and sorry self-talk stories

Explosions

Catastrophising

Self put-downs

Judging &
blaming

Idolising

Super self-talk stories

Time

Place

Cause

Ruminating

C = Consequence

D = Dispute

Any evidence?

Any alternative?

Does it help?

Does it matter?

E = Energise

Take action

Feelings are infectious. You can spread infectious optimism by using the same principles with team- or organisation-talk. Here are some opportunities to influence and help other people.

Relationships

Listen with empathy, and be an unreasonable friend. Act as a catalyst for happier living.

Leadership

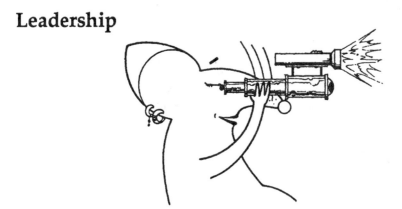

Inspire your group or team with an optimistic vision of the future. Use these skills to create a positive culture around you.

Team work

Listen to the team-talk. Then distract and dispute pessimistic explanations of events. Shift the team-talk to solving problems rather than ruminating over misery. Drive a new team-talk story.

Network marketing

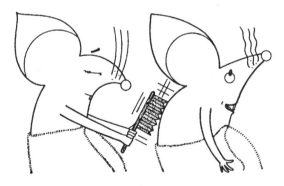

Encourage people in your network as they experience the inevitable frustrations in sponsoring and sales. Help them stay optimistic about the long-term future of their business.

Selling

Pessimistic sellers don't find many buyers. It's a self-fulfilling belief. If you're a seller, listen to your self-talk. The first step to increasing sales is shifting your thinking and beliefs towards optimism.

Sport

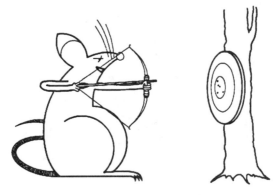

In competitive sports the optimistic players are more likely to succeed. When losing is looming, distract and dispute catastrophising and stay on target.

Get started now!

Remember from Chapter 1 that over half of our personality comes from our environment and experiences. We've got lots of opportunity to change ourselves. We're not solid rock.

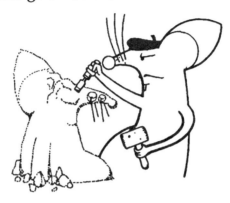

It takes practice to adopt and perfect new skills. Optimistic thinking is no different. It takes practice too.

So get started now!

Positively Optimistic

References

Bandler, Richard. *Using Your Brain - for a Change*. Moab, Utah: Real People Press, 1985.

Birch, Charles. *Feelings*. Sydney: University of New South Wales Press, 1995.

Ellis, Albert & Robert A. Harper. *A New Guide to Rational Living*. Hollywood, CA: Wilshire Book Company, 1975.

Goleman, Daniel. *Emotional Intelligence*. London: Bloomsbury Publishing Plc, 1996.

Maslow, Abraham H. *Motivation and Personality*. New York, NY: Harper Collins, 1970.

Maultsby, Maxie C. *Help yourself to happiness through rational self-counseling*. Boston: Marlborough House, 1975.

McCarthy, Michael J. *Mastering the Information Age*. Los Angeles: Jeremy P. Tarcher, Inc, 1991.

McLaughlin, Shirley. *The Driving Force*. Adelaide, SA, Australia: Angus & Robertson, 1995.

Rogers, Carl R. *On Becoming a Person*. London: Constable and Company, 1967.

Seligman, Martin E.P. *Learned Optimism.* Milsons Point, NSW, Australia: Random House, 1991.

Seligman, Martin E.P. *What You Can Change and What You Can't.* Milsons Point, NSW, Australia: Random House, 1994.

Wetzston, Ross. "Winning Ugly", *Inside Sports.* September, 1995.

Witmer, Melvin J. *Pathways to Personal Growth.* Muncie, Indiana: Accelerated Development Inc., 1985.

Index

Positively Optimistic

Spread the word

Bring Dr Ian McLean into your organisation to help spread the word about optimism, hope and persistence.

You'll get world-class content that your people can use immediately. And it's presented so they'll remember and act. There's heaps of participation with real learning.

You can book Ian for:

Conferences and workshops

*   Conference keynote presentations
*   Workshop facilitator

Meetings with your people

*   Sales meetings
*   Team meetings
*   Leadership training meetings

Building customer relationships

*   Breakfast or evening presentations to help you build relationships with clients

Ian has spoken to audiences in Australia, Europe, North America, Asia and Africa. When you book him you get credibility, experience and positive outcomes.

Notes

Notes